A Distant Reality

A Distant Reality
Poems

Marina E. Michaels

Athena Star Press

Copyright 2022 Marina E. Michaels

All rights reserved. No part of this publication may be reproduced, distributed, or transmitted in any form by any means, including photocopying, recording, or other electronic methods, without the prior written permission of the author, except for brief quotations embodied in reviews and certain other noncommercial uses permitted by copyright law. For permission requests, write to the publisher.

Athena Star Press
2467 Westvale Court
Santa Rosa, California 95403
athenastarpress.com
publisher@athenastarpress.com

Library of Congress Control Number: 2022904258

Paperback: 978-1-60038-005-1

EPUB: 978-1-60038-006-8

Kindle/Mobi: 978-1-60038-008-2

Printed in the United States of America with chlorine-free ink and on acid-free interior paper stock supplied by a provider certified by the Forest Stewardship Council.

First edition April 22, 2022

Contrary to what T.S. Eliot said, April is not the cruelest month. It's more like Chaucer with its shoures soote (showers sweet).

Cover and interior design: Marina E. Michaels

Title fonts: Darjeeling and Darjeeling Regnaments by FaceType

Copyright page, body text, poems, and notes fonts: Jos Buivenga's full-featured, dyslexia-friendly Museo and Museo Sans.

All images © Can Stock Photo. Cover: Stonehenge by mpanch. Introduction: Stonehenge by rolffimages. Exploring the edges of reality: Chichen Itza by Konstik. Inner space: composite of Sphinx and Small Magellanic Cloud by xfargas, using NASA images. Earth, ocean, and sky: Moai, Isla De Pascua, Rapa Nui by VKrupenkin. Stones in the earth: Petra by RuslanKphoto. Stories and storytellers: ancient Greek amphitheater, Taormina, Sicily. Poems for my children: Terracotta warriors of Xian by LaBamba. Friends, family, and lovers: First Nations petroglyphs, Utah by MikeNorton. Cycles and circles: Castlerigg stone circle, England by PhilBird. Juvenilia: The Kelpies, Falkirk, Scotland by SteveAllen. Translation: Karlevi runestone, Sweden by olandsfokus.

Contents

Introduction 1

Exploring the edges of reality 7
    Remembering the Future 9
    Spinning on the Edge of Time 10
    It's a game we play 11
    Rising Fire 12
    Memory Blast 13
    The Past 14
    Dry Times 15
    Magic 16
    Zero Hour 17

Inner space 19
    Taliesen's Sister 20
    Full Moon No More 21
    Barking at the Alamo 22
    The Assassin's Bullet 23
    The Blue Fairy 24
    Quietly Human 25
    Shark's Teeth 27
    Flee, Chiefs 28
    Caravan: A Poem on a Journey 29
    Dark Clouds in Tucson 31

Earth, ocean, and sky 33
    Sonnet to a Young Cat 34
    Red Riding Hood 35
    Creation 36
    Haiku For My Cat 37
    Breath of the Desert 38
    Desert Sunset 39
    Halloween 40

Desert Sunrise. 41
Renewal 42
New Homes Too Soon. 43
Time Slip 44
Dust Storm. 45
Earthquake. 46
Japanese Bobtails. 47
Cat on the Keyboard 48
Stickers and Thorns 49
Earth Magic 50
Wild Parrots. 51
Silent, still, the mummy sleeps 52
On the death of a kitten, ten months old 53
Pyramids 55
Air 56

Stones in the earth 57

On Essence 58
Physics Up and Down 59
Britain. 60
Psychic Radar 61
The Pleasure I Take 62
Half Dome in Winter. 63
Half Dome Two 64
To All of You: You Know Who You Are (Or Do You?) . 65
Reorientation. 66
Missing Persons 67
Changing Lines. 68
Changeling Lines 69
Fireworks 70
Meeting of Minds 71
Pretending 72
A Mother's Love 73

Stories and storytellers. 75

White Stone Weekend 76
One More River 78
Transformavit 80
Samurai 82
The Redeeming Factor. 83
Talking to myself. 85
Time Travelers. 86
Xanthippe. 87

Contents

    The Statue 88
    Cassandra 90

Poems for my children 91

    Second Story Cat 92
    The Smiling Bear 93
    Why Snakes Should Not Wear Ties 94

Friends, family, and lovers 97

    Love's Labor Lost 99
    Storm 100
    Shadow 101
    A.J.M. 102
    Silence in the Tropics 103
    Moon Song 104
    Summer Honey (for James Torrens, SJ) 105
    Mirror 106
    Galahad the Unchanging 107
    Sorcerer 109
    Sorceress-Shapechanger 110
    Fool's Gold 111
    Leavetaking 112
    Heart's Sister (for Kathe) 114
    False Dawn 115
    Touch of Kings 116
    Light and Shadow 117
    Possessions 118
    Soul Poisoner 119
    Good-bye, Adventurer 120
    Shining Sun 121
    The Trap 122
    Clear Water 123
    Shattered Mirrors 124
    To a Little Green Snake in the Grass 125
    The Fire at Midnight 126
    Refreshment 127
    Waiting for Him 128
    The Ten of Swords Looks for the Easy Out 129
    Wrapped in arms 130
    Relationships 131
    Long she wept by the sea 132
    The Ghosts of Never 133

Cycles and circles 135

    Phoenix Rising. 136
    Phoenix Flies 137
    Love Dawns. 138
    The Past Is Released. 139
    Hope Is Renewed 140
    Magical Salmon. 141
    00: The Wizard's Cast 142
    Haiku on the Hunter and the Hunted. 143
    The Falconer 144
    The Falconer II 145
    The Debt 146
    The Hounds. 148
    The Effrontery of Time 149
    Wild Mustard I 150
    Wild Mustard II 151
    Wild Mustard III. 152
    Wild Mustard IV. 153
    Wild Mustard V 154

Juvenilia 155

    Diamonds in the Rough. 156
    The Kiss 157
    Driftwood 158
    The Replacement 159
    Shoshannah in Winter 160
    Phoenix Lays an Egg 161
    Song of a Psychology Student 162
    Realization. 163
    Vice Versa 164
    Companions 165
    Anniversary of Realization. 166
    His Song. 167
    To the King of Beasts 168
    A Welcome and Invitation 169
    Words. 170
    The Persistence of Love. 171
    Fallen Star 172

Translation 173

    The Battle of Brunanburh (translation) 175
    The Battle of Brunanburh (original) 177

Introduction

My poems are snapshots of my interior state at the time I wrote them—truer than any photograph, more revealing, richer in communication, yet compact, weighing nothing, completely and permanently portable.

I've been urged by those few to whom I have shown my poetry, some of whom were well-known poets, to share my poems with a wider audience. It's taken me decades to muster the courage to do so.

As with all poetry, not every poem will speak to every person, and some poems may say something I didn't realize was there. Nor is every poem "good" from an objective point of view. But they are mine, and enough are good enough to share. The rest are here for completeness. I mean, what poet doesn't want to hold a slim volume containing their entire life's work to date? I have the skills and technology to make that happen.

I hope you enjoy enough of my poems to make this book worthwhile to you.

If you want, you can stop reading now and skip to the poems, which are organized loosely by theme. The rest of this introduction talks about how I write poems, what I believe poems are, why I think poetry is important, and why I titled this book *A Distant Reality*.

Poems are intensely personal

Unless a poem has been written as an exercise for the intellect, or as humor, or for a specific genre, such as children's poetry (and sometimes even under those circumstances), all poems are personal. That is, most poems come out of personal experiences the poet hopes to make universal. The best poems come out of that deeply creative part of ourselves connected to our greater whole. More on that source in a bit.

Not counting my translation of the old English poem, *The Battle of Brunanburh* (which you can find in the last chapter), the poems in this book arise out of that creative space. For me, that space is also where I *feel* the most, meaning where I also feel the most vulnerable.

So I have a hard time sharing my poems. A rejecting word directed at my poetry is a word directed at my innermost self. I shrivel inside and retreat from the rejection. Reject me, reject my innermost truth. Likewise, an encouraging word sustains me.

As a consequence, I rarely share my poetry with anyone, and over time I've deleted many poems that were too personal, and that therefore I felt spoke to no one but myself. I'm now strong enough that I feel comfortable in sharing my poems, and I can accept that people might not understand the poems, or me, or might reject who I am. That's okay. Though it's hard to believe, even the beloved Mr. Rogers had his critics.

My poems come from other realities

If you write poetry, you're a poet. Don't let anyone dissuade you. It doesn't matter whether you're objectively "good" at it. And it doesn't matter how you write them. You write poetry? You're a poet.

Every poet has a different way of writing poetry, though broadly speaking people use one of two ways to write their poems, or a combination of the two. They either plan their poems before writing them, or they write their poems as the poems come to them, sometimes starting with one line and letting the poem flow creatively and spontaneously from there.

I mostly use the second method, with a bit of the first.

It's a mystery to me how most of my poems were inspired and written, and sometimes in what they are about.

I write most of my poetry through a cooperative creative process in which a two-way communication takes place, a process in which a poem is conveyed to me in one form and then I translate it into another. On one end of that two-way communication is the poet. The other end is a creative source, which I don't venture to define beyond saying that it is vastly creative and immensely loving.

That source has sustained me through the years, with brief but important messages from beyond the normal bounds of reality, messages conveyed in words and rhythms that have meaning within the constraints of everyday reality. Hence the book's title, *A Distant Reality*: Many of my poems bring information from one reality to another, and are native to that border that lies between those realities.

Introduction

Because I believe that the creative source that I listen to is in great part a co-creator and co-writer with me, I also believe that many of these poems contain deeper messages than I may not yet be aware of.

Sometimes I've only figured out years later what a poem meant; either as explication of what was going on in my life at the time, or as a prediction of what was yet to come.

Some poems are deceptively simple on the surface, but can bring you back again and again, tantalized by some thought or impression that whisks away just out of reach, teasing you, luring you down a path that may bring unforeseen delights.

If so, then I am happy that, in having shared my poetry, I may have helped someone remember the magic in life.

My writing process

As with my writing, my poetry process is mostly listening to a creative source and writing down, however imperfectly, what I think I am hearing.

In this listening, some of my poems have come to me entire and whole—say, in a dream or while daydreaming. Others have come to me in part—I'll hear or see or feel the first few lines arriving, line by line, as I fall asleep, or while I am driving or doing something else unrelated to writing poetry. Then I must stop what I'm doing and write those first lines immediately, and listen closely to an inner sense to come up with the remainder of the poem. I've learned that if I don't start writing the poem immediately, the thoughts and words go away forever.

So I write down what I remember, then compose the rest of the poem based on the mood and sense of what it is I (or whoever) was trying to say.

Sometimes, in the process of composing, I return to the creative, listening state well enough to get a closer approximation of the original poem. Other times, I am not quite so lucky, and then the composition is more a product of my creative, intuitive self and my rational mind working together to come up with something that is good poetry on both the evocative side and the more linear "but is it poetry?" side, and that retains the original poem's feeling and meaning.

A few times, several poems have come to me in a quick creative burst. Once, for example, I wrote three sonnets and most of a fourth in fifteen minutes. They came to me as swiftly as I could write them down—almost as though someone were dictating them to me. And perhaps someone was.

Like the nettle shirts woven by the young Lisa in the fairy tale (to turn her swan brothers back into their human form), the fourth sonnet was incomplete. I was interrupted, the flow stopped, and I never completed that fourth sonnet. A few days later, I "got" one more complete sonnet; an afterthought, perhaps, of whatever creative process was at work.

I find that such poems resist editing, as though their perceived imperfections contain some seed of truth that would not otherwise be present if I made them more logical and understandable.

I don't write all my poems this way, but that's how I wrote most of my favorites. I will venture to say that if you ask some of the best writers (of any form—poetry, fiction, even non-fiction), you will find that they, too, obtained much of their inspiration through listening to an interior voice.

How and why I arranged the poems

Most books of poetry by a single author present the poems in chronological order. Or a poet publishes chaplets—small books with just a handful of poems on a single theme or from a span of years.

At one time I arranged my poetry chronologically too. However, eventually I asked myself, "In what other ways, perhaps more meaningful ways, could I organize my poems?"

The organization I came up with—a loose organization by theme—represents only one answer to that question. I could organize these poems in a variety of different ways, all of them with something to offer. Each form of organization I could choose would be like turning a kaleidoscope—the poems fall into new patterns, new ways of being seen, complemented in different ways by the poems around them, like jewels in different settings.

And of course, many of the poems don't fall neatly into one category. For example, the poem "Earth Magic" in the chapter "Earth, ocean, sky" could have as easily gone into "Exploring the edges of reality" or "Inner space." Even as I made my final editing pass, I stopped and pondered the placement of some poems. In the end, I left them organized as is.

In some ways, organizing poems in any other way than chronological runs the risk of people categorizing them too strongly as one type of poem, or perhaps overlooking some poems because they are in the "wrong" chapter, or missing the finer nuances and possible ways of looking at them because the poems are labeled, and labels affect perception.

But since the intention behind this book is to share what I have experienced of this grand reality we call our home, it is my hope that, however you come to them, the poems in this book speak to you and bring light on your path and, when appropriate, joy to your heart, and a smile to your lips.

Introduction

Do poems need commentary?

It's been the fashion for many decades, if not centuries, to publish poems without commentary. The idea is that a good poem speaks for itself, and one shouldn't draw attention to the bad ones. I agree with that philosophy to a certain extent.

I don't believe it's right to tell people what they should think of a poem, or what they should get out of it. For one thing, different people get different things out of a poem, sometimes different things from the same poem at different times. And sometimes people find in a poem things the poet never saw, but that are indisputably there once noticed.

For the most part, I've avoided this kind of commentary; that is, I've avoided telling people what they should get out of my poems.

And yet I've added comments to most of my poems. Why? It enriches a poem to know something about its context—the experiential bed out of which the poem arose, the surroundings in the poet's life within which the poem grew.

I also believe that perhaps one of the biggest barriers to enjoying poetry is not having enough information to enjoy that poetry. It can be off-putting to be told, "if you don't understand it without commentary, you don't deserve to read it." Which can put off some people enough that they vow to never read any poetry.

But everyone loses in that scenario—the poets lose a chance to share their message, and the people who reject all poetry lose a way to add richness and variety and wonder to their lives.

So I've added commentary to many of my poems, striving to walk that fine line between over-explication and absolute mystery. Mostly, I talk about a poem's context and let the poem speak for itself. If I make a literary reference, I might explain that part. That way, those reading this book can choose which poems to take away with them in their hearts without feeling as though I have told them too much.

I hope some of these poems will touch you in some way, will bring you a new perspective or that "ah ha!" feeling. Perhaps it will help to know that someone else has had similar experiences. Perhaps you will smile on reading one of my poems, or laugh, even, or in some way find that the poem and you have met in that spiritual space, your heart.

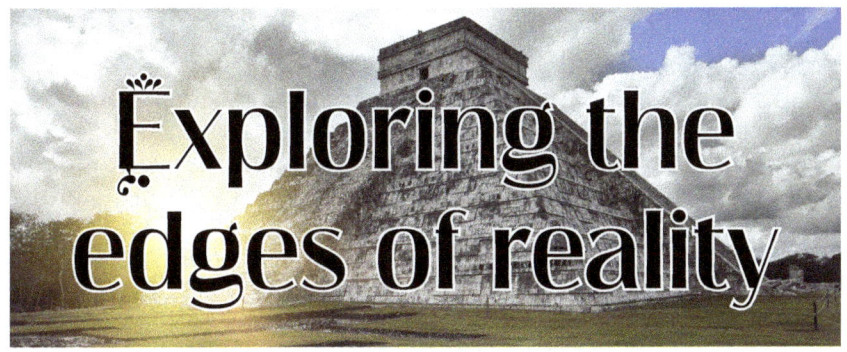

Exploring the edges of reality

Life isn't as neatly packaged and explainable as many of us would like to think. There is something more beyond what we see, and, depending on how we think, we sometimes catch glimpses of that reality. How willing are we to not have control? How much uncertainty are we willing to accept in our lives? How willing are we to let people and things be whoever or whatever they are that day, without insisting that they conform to some standard we've set or some previous expectations we've created for them? Is that coffee table truly and always a coffee table, or is it something more, or different, when you're not looking?

The more open we are to uncertainty, the more we can see things as they are and not as we wish them to be.

One way to look at it is in terms of accepting gifts from the ocean. Let's say we collect seashells. In our search, some of us stay in one very specific part of just one beach, insisting that we will only look in that spot for the shells we want. And furthermore, we have a list, right here, that says what shells we think we need for our collection, and what shells we expect to find on this portion of the beach. If we find a different shell, we reject it because it isn't on our list. We might not even see some shells because we are so focused on looking for only the shells that match our list, and we don't think it is possible for new, other kinds of shell to be there.

We can miss a lot of beautiful seashells that way.

And too often we don't think to visit another part of the beach, let alone another beach entirely, where other shells might wait, if we aren't finding the shells we want. Our lives are that much poorer for this attitude.

The more willing we are to accept whatever the sea brings us that day, and the more willing we are to try different beaches (and to examine unexpected shells), the more able we are to experience whatever magic is going on around us at any minute. And that's where many of my poems, in this book and especially in this chapter, have arisen from: experiencing the magic of a moment.

The first poem in this chapter compactly summarizes this idea. Like many of my poems, it came to me in a different state of consciousness than waking reality. In this case, I received it in a dream many levels of reality away from this one, and had to stop at each level on my journey back to my home reality, "waking up" within another dream, to translate the poem into the language and concepts of that level before proceeding with the poem to the next level closer to my home reality, where I repeated the translation process one last time when I woke up in this reality.

It was much like carrying a small basket of precious eggs while hopping and jumping over rocks and streams. In this case, some eggs were lost, falling to the rocks, but most of the meaning (the essential eggieness) remained. So consider that poem as a translation of a translation of a translation: the essence is there, even though not in its the original form.

The other poems in this chapter follow the same theme: There is something more beyond what we see, and sometimes we catch a glimpse of that reality beyond.

Exploring the edges of reality

Remembering the Future

Wandering toward the fire
They wonder at the distance.
Wonder holds their breaths
As jugglers perform.
Despite constrictions appear
Multitudinous wonders.

Go no further, fear says,
Speak of only safe things.

Voyages are made despite the fear.

Go beneath the surface
Rise above the air
There's something there
Fair. It speaks:
Abandon fear. Embrace wonder.
Venture for yourselves to find the sea.
You are free.

September 9, 1981

I was given this poem in a dream within a dream within a dream within a dream (and so on, for about five levels of dreams). As I "woke" from each dream into the next, I translated the poem into the language of that new reality. Finally I woke in this reality and transcribed what I had retained. The poem, "Caravan: A Poem on a Journey" on page 29 is the next step in the journey this poem began.

Spinning on the Edge of Time

Midnight, and she awakes
From restless dreams of magic states
And drifts through darkly starlit halls
And feels the wind blow through the walls
Until stark silence fills all space
And blurs the edges of her face.
Eroding winds blow through her cells
And carry her away.

April 15, 1982
I wrote most of a short story, "The Miller's Son," a retelling of Puss in Boots, in the middle of the night with no memory of having done so. But there it was in my handwriting when I woke that morning. Still in a dreamy state, I wrote this poem.

Exploring the edges of reality

It's a game we play

It's a game we play;
The knowledge from other lives
Echoes, ignored, in our minds
We pretend there is only this once
And never again
To learn the entire world and its meaning
To swallow down until it becomes us
And breathes out again from every cell, singing.

July 8, 1982
Based on a momentary memory from a related life.

Rising Fire

The stars.
The stars are not dead.
They live and breathe fire
They talk to each other in a communion
no person ever knew
Until I came along.
Their fierce strength vibrates in my bones
And delight fills my soul
As my heart opens, expanding to fill the universe
Until I *am* the universe.

And when I return to earth
The fire of the distant stars
Their love and pride
And sureness
Glow in my eyes
for all to see and share.
The fire spreads
Until each person knows
That we are all stars too.

November 3, 1984
Written in a workshop. I've long forgotten the workshop's details.

Memory Blast

Fast
Bar my tongue from speaking
An ancient terror
That you haven't lived yet.
I've seen the horror,
Lived it
And as my ghost screams by
Helplessly caught in a time wind
Across your sun-drenched and uncaring stone
Only a few look up, take heed, and shiver
in the final summer's complacent heat.

July 22, 1990

Written after a harrowing trip on the astral plane to a summer in the peaceful time of an ancient civilization right before disaster struck.

The Past

It's a country I've sailed far from
Its customs, its boundaries
Are shrinking
And still the ice wind fills my sails
And drives me on.

September 8, 1990
We leave the past behind us, but what happened then can still drive us.

Dry Times

He lives in a dead world
The sticks and stones speak
But he hears only silence
And a vast dry wind that blows all help away.

November 2, 1990
Some people live in a dead world and pity those of us who speak with rocks. In the end, who is the richer? Who the poorer?

Magic

Beneath ordinary flesh
The sleek slippery sea otter
Builds bones of royal purple.

August 3, 1992
When I discovered that sea otters have purple bones,
I knew life had more magic in store for us all.

Zero Hour

And Now is the moment
When All
That ever was
Or ever will be

Is.

May 11, 1995
I am not the first nor will be the last to say that Now is the pivotal moment upon which the past and future rely.

Inner space

In discovering who I am in this life, I've had to learn the balance between allowing life as it is and setting limits. Because of things that happened in my childhood, I used to allow others to take advantage of me. Because I know how it feels to be forced into situations I did not want to be in, I've had a lifelong visceral horror of ever placing anyone else in the same position. That meant I often would bend over backwards to avoid the appearance of coercion, and would end up giving others far too much room, and not keeping nearly enough space for myself to live in.

Experiencing life in that open-ended way has given me a unique perspective; nonetheless, I wouldn't want to return to that way of being. In living through those times, I produced some of my best poetry, as my inner wisdom tried to tell me to find balance, and to dare to see that some people were not good for me.

I didn't fully understand some of my poetry when I wrote it; I needed the perspective gained from experience to fully grasp what my poetry-writing self was trying to tell me.

As someone recently said, "Givers must set limits because takers never will." That is, you can give and give and give until, exhausted, you have nothing left to give, and some people will still keep taking from you. Once you set boundaries and limits, they vanish to find another easy mark.

The poems in this chapter were written while I was learning who I am and becoming more myself. As Carl Jung once said, we can have a shadow of light as well as of dark. I once thought myself all dark, but have come to a more balanced opinion.

Taliesen's Sister

I am a pond
Covered with leaves
And no wind to scatter them.

I am a mermaid that rises from the seas
Seen as a narwhal
Ugly and common.

I am a pyramid
Secrets locked in my chambered heart
The spoken key forgotten.

I am a cloud drifting
All things to all people
Mist and cold air to myself.

I am Taliesen's sister
Magic and strong
Knowing myself
Unknown.

December 3, 1983
Sometimes I think poems slide, sideways, out of other dimensions and times into our own pasts, and wait there for us to discover them. I generally have an excellent memory of my poems (not the exact words, necessarily, but the poem's existence, yes). This poem, however, I found intact in an old dream journal, more than ten years after writing it, written in my handwriting, without anything crossed out. I had never recorded it anywhere else, and I had no memory of writing it. I think it was just waiting to be rediscovered when I was ready to hear its message.

Inner space

Full Moon No More

I've tasted the wolf's tongue between my teeth
Felt the sharp hot saliva
Dripping
As I've raced
Solitary
But with the pack in my mind
Until we tore down and savaged
Our latest quarry.

I know the hunt
From both sides
And when hunted
Or when disinterested, already full
With some other triumph
I've scorned it, been better
than the hunters.

Now: I look full on
and pull my tongue back in
My teeth grow shorter
Duller
And my ears, no longer furred
Round to my skull.
And I am human.

March 9, 1990

Written a few years before Clarissa Pinkola Estes' Women Who Run With the Wolves, *this poem has gotten strong reactions from men. This poem is, in part, about some of my related lifetimes, and also, in part, about how it is possible to be savage and yet scorn savagery at the same time. In some ways, it is about what it might mean to be a werewolf in the modern day, and the savage angry impulse behind the attacks people feel free to make on the Internet. And it is about how eventually, when one arrives at a peace within oneself, the savage impulse is no more, or is at least under one's control. A human being is, in this context, a fully realized soul who does not engage in violent acts except when justified defending self and others. "Quietly Human" on page 25 continues this theme.*

Barking at the Alamo

That dark dog
Shadow-caught and remarkable
His tenacious body holds
strength in every lean cell.

Swimming with the river
One with the tide
He knows an identity
I don't.

April 18, 1990
One of my all-time favorite poems. It started to come to me line by line as I was falling asleep; I forced myself to get up and write it down. It doesn't seem perfect to me, but every effort I have made to make it a "better" poem in the conventional sense has been resisted by that inner guidance that I have learned to listen to.

Inner space

The Assassin's Bullet

You can fear it all your life
And never feel it.
You can hear it past your ear
And never die.

May 21, 1991

This poem came to me in a dreamy state at the exact time that Rajiv Gandhi was assassinated by a suicide bomber, though I only heard the news hours later. Rajiv, then Prime Minister of India, was Indira Gandhi's son. Indira had been assassinated in 1984. There was more to the poem, but when I forced myself more fully awake to write it down, this was all I could remember. I later decided to incorporate this poem into "Caravan: A Poem on a Journey" on page 29; the styles and content are compatible.

The Blue Fairy

Pinocchio's sister
A woman of wood
Waiting to turn into something real
All the slow years
Whittling away at the wooden numbness
Not even a Pleasure Island to break the gloom
Until finally awareness dawns.

August 3, 1992
Most people don't get this one. I'll say this much: The awareness (represented by the Blue Fairy) that dawns is the knowledge that she is already real.

Quietly Human

I have experienced beauty so rich
that all my senses weren't enough
so I developed more

I have felt despair so deep—
no one to turn to,
no aid around—
that I wanted to wither.
But a life depended on me
so I developed more

I have been plain and ordinary
Striking and strange.

I have romped with children,
I have convened with adults.

I have known the freedom of not caring what others think,
and I have known the strictures of fear
that hobbled my expression
so that all anyone saw
were the most superficial and least likable parts of me.
And I have seen the harm to my spirit
And I developed more:

A deep knowledge of the value of life
and of living your own life;
An understanding that we are all alone,
and all in this together;
That sometimes integrity demands
that we stand against all opposition,
and other times group good demands
submergence of the individual's needs.

The fine balance between,
the knowing of which to do when
is all part of the process
of becoming
quietly
human.

A Distant Reality

November 18, 1992
This poem continues the theme from "Full Moon No More" on page 21. Being human includes, not the lack of our stronger emotions, but control over them.

Shark's Teeth

Shark's teeth
Disorderly and deadly
Give my submerged mind
A message
It fails to grasp

Only the slow-swaying kelp
Heeds my screams.

September 1993
Sometimes we trap ourselves in situations that kill us slowly.

Flee, Chiefs

Flee, chiefs
Even from doctors
Some deposit and
Some buy
And some are caught
between.
Digging sand is hard—
But try growing in it.

April 16, 1994
This poem came completely from that creative source I spoke of in the introduction. I like it, despite its obscurity.

Inner space

Caravan: A Poem on a Journey

The assassin's bullet.
> You can fear it all your life
> And never feel it.
> You can hear it past your ear
> And never die.

It lurches into action.
> See the fear. See it,
> But do not yield.
>
> Fine deeds, like fine thoughts,
> require focus, balance, intention.

A viewpoint.
> To venture in this world
> is to see
> Good, bad, indifferent
> and be free
> of judgments, but not taste.

The watering hole.
> Choose well. Then choose again,
> if choosing any action causes pain.

An oasis.
> Romany rests.
> But were the King of the Roma here today
> (And is he not?)
> His comment to the world might be
> Be merry, and be free
> Explore your inner realm, that inner sea.
> Seek inner hosts; dance and play
> 'Til lightness fills your heart, and love,
> And freedom chases fear away.

April 28, 1995
The "on a journey" part of this poem's title means two things. The poem is about a journey, and the poem itself is in the process of be-

coming. It also relates to and follows "Remembering the Future" on page 9 and "The Assassin's Bullet" on page 23. The "it" lurching into action in the second verse is the caravan.

Inner space

Dark Clouds in Tucson

In some places
It is always dark
And the sun never rises
Daylight knocks
And goes away unwanted.
Invited only are those dark birds
Despair
And Hunger
And the only change is from one grey to another.

And even if the sun somehow shines more brightly than gloom's worst fears
It doesn't take much work to close one's eyes.

November 18, 1999
Written on some impulse arising out of I knew not where at the time. Why the title? Tucson is a bright and sunny city, and even though it has its own dark (and magnificent) storms, it is quite hard to pretend that all is dreary there. Yet some people manage to.

Earth, ocean, and sky

It has been a philosophical fashion for thousands of years to abnegate the flesh; to declare "Woe is me for being in a physical body!" (I'm side-eying you, Gnosticism), and to long for existence as a "pure" spirit. Some view this belief as a way to control people, because how more trapped can you be, spiritually speaking, than to inhabit a body you cannot escape, a body whose very nature, you are told, is foul pollution?

Even before I came to believe in loving Creators who most definitely wouldn't give us bodies and a physical world as some form of punishment for crimes only we humans imagined, I believed physical reality was made to enjoy as we learn to be better humans. We can take great joy in everyday things without feeling guilty—a small flower, a kitten's arching sideways playful dance, the taste of a perfect dessert.

I believe that all that has been created out of love is meant to be loved; believing that we have loving Creators means that whatever we perceive as loving is what we will receive.

Many of these poems arose out of that belief, and a joy in everyday things.

Sonnet to a Young Cat

Unmoving, still, my Snuffbox (orange-striped cat)
Is posed as if forgetting why he stood.
Some weighty matter (like his saucer's milk)
Has sudden forced itself into his mind.
But no, he sits again and licks his paw
Then raises it to wash behind his ear
Uncaring that my interest he has raised
Or caring much: he wants me not to know
What cat-like business wrought the rapid change
From basalt stillness to the liquid flow
Of cat on bed to cat standing on floor.
Perhaps the thought was gone when full he woke.
    Dream thoughts are often thus so quickly lost,
    And trouble many greater with the cost.

1976
First published in Cats *magazine, November 1976.*

Red Riding Hood

She could have been talking about kittens
That long-ago girl amazed at the size
God graced wolf's ears with.
Staring me in the face in the morning
Kittens make me wonder too.
Are those small heads all cavity?
The illusion is emphasized
By wide, pink, teeth-clicking yawns
But dispelled by the mobile alertness
Of those keen, twitching ears
And of the round wide eyes
That follow every movement of mine.

May 1978
Kittens. Endless variety, endless enjoyment.

Creation

God drew a circle
Sketched in quick fine details—
Whiskers
Triangle nose
Slant eyes
Long tail curled round half the form.
Then
Breathed a Word
And the form uncurled
Yawned
Stretched
Became Cat.

January 1979
One might start to detect a theme here. Do I like cats? Oh, yes, I do!

Haiku For My Cat

Rubbed and sleek, this cat
Resembles fine polished wood—
But moves like water.

October 8, 1980

Breath of the Desert

Breath of the desert
Smells richly of wet earth
Speaks of life thriving, surviving
Harsh heat
Because of purple lightning
Gentle rain.

The wet cat in the window
Jumps down and shakes herself.

September 1, 1981
Though I long ago put down roots in Northern California's lush wine country, I sometimes miss the Arizona high desert, where I lived from 1981 to 1988.

Desert Sunset

Chiseled mountains stark against the sky
Strike inward to the unresisting heart
Which, slowly sinking, joins the brilliant sun
Until the vision sets within the mind:
Rough outline filled with insubstantial motes
Of lavender, like shining worlds remote
And dancing, at the same time seems so flat,
A knife's edge, as it slowly fades to black.
Sharp cutout black against a fiery orange.
Then nothing, but two stars which pierce the eyes
And dare the stricken heart to turn away.

October 9, 1981
Desert sunsets can be spectacular—and magical.

Halloween

Counting kittens' ribs
Or their tails' rings;
Smoothing semi-gloss fur,
Fine and warm as down,
Pumpkin orange or charcoal black;
Not much else to do when kittens sleep on you
But smile and wonder
Whether the world has room
For such innocence.

October 29, 1981
Kittens. How can anyone deal with them cruelly? Robert Heinlein once said that there is a special place in Hell reserved for people who harm kittens, and Sir Terry Pratchett said the same in his Discworld *series. And although I believe in forgiveness and the lack of Hell, I'd be tempted to make an exception in this case. There's a place right next to it reserved for those who harm children. Except I also believe in infinite Divine mercy and love.*

Desert Sunrise

Watch the sun rise
In a wine glass.
Its patient radiance
Spreads slowly up the curves.
Above, the capsuled sky,
Gray, growing blue,
Encircles an advertisement
Chased with leaves. I think
Even the Original Artists
Would be amused.

November 16, 1981

This poem was written after watching a desert sunrise through a wine glass with a restaurant's logo on it, thinking how amusing it might be to our Creators to see their incomparable work surrounded by an advertisement, as though the makers of the glass could somehow claim credit for the sunrise.

Renewal

Let the desert wind blow through you
Let the rocks and sand grow to you
Stretch out your arms and feel your skin grow thick.

Let the sun's bright heat become you
As you let yourself succumb to
The knowledge you are part of all that is.

January 7, 1982
A kind of prayer and hope. I was so lost when living in the desert. And yet it is also where I started to get unlost.

New Homes Too Soon

Hunting in corners
Peering anxiously under the couch
And calling
Calling.

Hormones, he says, just hormones.
She didn't show this much care
When they were here.

Finally she settles by the aquarium.
Maybe she thinks her kittens
Have turned into fish.

December 16, 1982
Written when, on bad advice, I gave my cat's kittens away sooner than I felt right.

Time Slip

Thou sleek, thou dragon-eyed cats,
Coats patched with shadows and moonlight
Whose hard strength slides,
Effortless as nightfall and the hunt,
Under fur, over bones
Of adamant, air-light:
You dance with time.

In another age
Scarlet dragons, scaled, sage
Make Men guess at the riddle whose answer lies
In the star-bright gleam of your cat eyes.

June 22, 1984
One of my personal all-time favorites. I don't recall, now, the circumstances of its writing, but I do know that it has resisted all attempts to edit it, even to "correct" the use of thou, which for many years I thought was supposed to refer only to the second person singular. More recent scholarship indicates that, in fact, thou was used for second-person plural, as well, giving further credence to the knowingness of that creative source from which this poem sprang.

Dust Storm

A dust wind rises
Sluggishly stirs
Coils sleepily around the desert hills
Strengthens
And winds its heart tighter into the heat.
Its scales scrape
Lift dry desert ground
Creating clouds
That wrap around the hills
And recreate them.

April 25, 1985
Seeing renewal in the desert helped me think that perhaps someday I would find my own renewal.

Earthquake

The earth shakes
and I with it
An inadvertent dance,
Each partner slightly out of step.
We both wonder
Will she make it?

May 1, 1990
I was living and working a few miles from the epicenter when the 1989 Loma Prieta earthquake struck. My life was very different afterward. It just took me a while to realize it.

Japanese Bobtails

Do they sometimes dream
of having a tail?
In their sleep do they chase
long sinuous ropes of fur?
Do they pin with one paw
this useful adjunct to their rear?
I see them rotate their little stubs
wildly for balance.
Do they know what's missing?
Do they care?

November 14, 1991

Japanese Bobtails have naturally short tails. They are charming cats, compact, great jumpers, elegant, intelligent, and conversant with humans.

Cat on the Keyboard

<F6> Delete all files?
No! Wait! That was my cat.

Too late.

And thus is havoc wrought
When all I sought
Was peace.

September 22, 1992
Anyone with cats and a computer knows what this poem is about. I was amused to discover that someone invented software called PawSense that detects patterns of "cat typing" on the keyboard to prevent just this kind of accident.

Stickers and Thorns

Needle-sharp teeth
Tiny, accurate, deadly
(To a moth, perhaps)
Tiny claws, the sharper for their smallness
Fur sticking straight out.

The stickers impale
The thorns sink in
I die! I die!

The smallness, triumphant
dances away
as lightly and as fragile
as leaves.

October 8, 1992
Because it hasn't been clear to some: this poem is about kittens.

Earth Magic

I once lay on the dark and dreaming earth
And felt its infinite support beneath
Pressing me up to the sky.

I felt the sun's strong warmth
Illuminate my cells
And kiss the earth beneath me with its light.

I heard the slight wings of gnats
And the vast conference of redwoods
And all good things between.

As I lay thus united
With the earth
And her magic,
I heard another sound:
The heckling of seagulls
The sardonic laughter of ducks.

January 28, 1994
There is a bit of my characteristic dry self-deprecating humor in this poem; a poking fun at taking anything, even a blissful connection with life, too seriously. The ducks and gulls are always there, ready to bring you back to earth with their gently mocking laughter.

Wild Parrots

I have seen the wild parrots swift in flight
A graceless bird on land transformed on wing
A triad's focused flight; a burst of green
A glimpse of other worlds, secret, unseen.

When wild parrots fly, the world turns green
And ordinary thoughts take magic flight
The air glows from within; supernal light
Indelibly inscribes this wild sight.

I blink; the birds are gone; did they exist?
Was this strange sight a message or a tryst
arranged to bring me hope by beings unseen?
Is magic in the world, and is it green?

November 25, 1998
I once saw three wild parrots flying swiftly and with purpose in formation over Stevens Creek Boulevard, a busy multilaned road in Cupertino, California (in the heart of Silicon Valley). Houses stretched for miles in all directions. It was a magical sight. The only conclusion I could draw was that the parrots or their parents had escaped from captivity and that a colony of parrots was thriving in the interstices of the urban environment.

Silent, still, the mummy sleeps

The body awaits renewal
silent, still,
dead to modern eyes,
but filled with joy and anticipation
against the call to rise.

Late 1990s/early 2000s
My daughter Elisabeth took down these words while I was talking in my sleep.

Earth, ocean, and sky

On the death of a kitten, ten months old

His strength is gone
He lies, too weak to move, staring
Side gently rising and falling
the only sign of life.

His spirit, strong and sad,
Asks me only
"Have I been a good boy?"
And the poignancy of all
That lies behind his thought
Ambushes my heart, and I am lost.

I rush to assure him
That his whole life was good
That it was I who failed him
Failed in faith
Failed in trust
Failed in love
And he falls silent.

I wait a while, and watch
His breathing still steady
And wonder how it is
That we in the world have so lost our faith
That a simple kitten, dying simply
("I want to go home," he said,
and showed me a vision
of him leaping in joy,
Effortless, free,
In some eternity beyond)
can bring so much sorrow
When instead perhaps we need to know
That for spirits, there is always tomorrow.

February 3, 2002

Lemon—that's the name he gave me, and I am sticking with it—came into our lives and left again within a year. Born in 2001 the day after my brother Peter's birthday, he was an elegant and aware kitten, in tune with everything, but always a little uncertain of himself. One day he sickened and there was nothing I could do. I stayed by his side as he breathed his last breaths. Farewell, sweet Lemon. All heart's ease to you.

Pyramids

What must they have looked like,
In their splendor, in their day?
Rising gladly in the hearts of those who saw them.
"We did this. We made that,"
And always in the eye
The pyramids outlined against the sky.

March 6, 2014
Inspired by a sudden mental image of looking in satisfaction at the newly constructed pyramids.

Air

Air moves softly against the skin
Unseen and unheard
Except when it collides with something else

Rising to gale forces
It can move mountains
And does
Unseen and unheard

July 30, 2015

Stones in the earth

Like the stones of the chapter's title, the poems in this chapter tell of people and experiences that can seem common, but on close examination are uniquely themselves.

On Essence

Water
Wanderer
Ripple
Whip-supple
Shape-changer
To suit circumstance.
In any guise
Recognized.

September 2, 1980
You could take this to be a comment on water. You could also take it to be a comment on those people who, chameleon-like, shift and change to adapt to their surroundings, sometimes in an attempt to hide or deceive. You could also conclude that, no matter what shape water takes, it is always recognizable.

Physics Up and Down

Six flavors of quarks—
How charming and strange. Beauty
At bottom and top.

October 12, 1980

Written when I learned that the quirky physicists had decided to call the six known attributes of quarks "flavors," and then had named those flavors up, down, charm, strange, bottom, and top. In order to get the flavors "up" and "down" into the poem, however, since it is a haiku, I added a title.

Britain

Black umbrellas and black cars
On the rain-darkened cobbled streets.
Black roofs above
Beneath a grey sky.

March 1982
An image from a related life, where all the cars and umbrellas in London, it seemed, were black. Perhaps the 1940s.

Psychic Radar

Incoming lies
Blips on the screen
Flying in low
Think they haven't been seen.

And they wouldn't be seen,
They'd get off scot-free
If it weren't for this radar
Here inside me.

October 20, 1984

In my past it often took me a while to listen to my intuition, but when I wrote this poem, I was starting to figure out how important it was to listen. It had never steered me wrong. I didn't and still don't usually let people know that I know they're lying; I just observe.

The Pleasure I Take

In people's faces
Has nothing to do with beauty
And everything.

October 24, 1986
The title contributes to the thought, and so this isn't a true haiku.

Stones in the earth

Half Dome in Winter

Round stone mountain hammered out of gold
Rising warm above the shivering cold
Snow-light plains and ice-dark water. Pines
Stand clustered thick in black forbidding lines,
With chilly fingers spread toward the sky,
While clouds in tatters through the thin air fly.
Above this space my heart goes sharply crying
Alone and lost, toward the seashore flying.
In cutting winds I dream of desert days
Of warmer friends, and warmer speaking ways.
Ahead I see a future crystal bright.
As frozen burdens melt, my heart grows light.
    It seems my life is fated to be this:
    Half ice-cold dreams, half hammered golden bliss.

December 13, 1988

Half Dome is a magnificent glacially carved stone mountain face in Yosemite, California, one of the lovelier of the many lovely places on earth. I wrote this sonnet the year I moved back to California after living in Tucson for seven years.

Half Dome Two

In empty space the seagull sharply cries
Alone and lost as now the cold light dies.
The seagull hastens on toward the sea.
It's dark. A bleak wind rushes through the trees.

Divided mountain, sky, divided mind
A heart in two, an eye that double finds.
Here lies the fight, the struggle to be free.
Dark and light contrast themselves for me:
A message from my heart that all is love;
That as it is below, so too above.

I know perception's touching madness deep
But struggle for the lighter touch: I keep
reminding self to discard this illusion
of enemies, brave souls in fell confusion.

Divided hearts rejoice when the light dies.
Alone and lost, the seagull fiercely cries.
But as I stumble yet again and fall,
My single heart tells me that love is all.

February 17, 1989
A continuation of "Half Dome in Winter" on page 63. Still iambic pentameter, but not a sonnet.

To All of You: You Know Who You Are (Or Do You?)

Okay
So I was naive beyond belief
and so you didn't believe it.
You, so smug in your chitinous, cynical armor
But I finally figured you out
All of you
It took me years sometimes
But I did
And all I have to say is
Sad
      Sad
            Sad
of you to have spurned
that which was most holy and innocent
in yourself.

February 11, 1989

Some people take pride in being smugly cynical and make fun of those who have a more optimistic and innocent approach to life.

Reorientation

My world spins again
Settles into a new position
Once again I stagger off balance a moment
An inadvertent dance that lands me on my feet.

February 20, 1989
Written during a rough period in my life. Which, come to think of it, means it could have been written any time in my life.

Missing Persons

Faces in the mail
Have you seen this child?
Stranger abduction
Ten years ago
And they're still looking—
They haven't given up hope.
The child is 18 or 20
Or more
Long ago resigned to its fate
Or dead
Or escaped
But certainly not where it was
Or whom
Those many years gone.

Faces on the street
Or at your office
Or even at home.
Whose child are they,
long ago abducted
from a fairy-tale life
by rough real parents?
Handled with impunity
And punished punished punished
For not vanishing.

April 15, 1992

This poem is about perhaps the biggest factor contributing to all the ills of society today: Children who have not been loved as they should have been. They may not have gone missing in the conventional sense, but they were lost nonetheless. Childhood trauma is far more common than many people know, and it affects people deeply and in different ways. Be kind and compassionate; you may not know what that person has experienced.

Changing Lines

To men: You express love
with urgent desire
to leave your way behind

but instead, your rapid want
leaves behind
the way of those you love.

May 21, 1992
The "changing lines" in the title refers to the I Ching, in which coins or yarrow stalk are tossed. Sometimes the results are called "changing lines," which means lines that are interpreted one way, and then are shifted (changed) and read in another way, sometimes giving a different meaning. So too this poem, which came purely and directly to me from that creative source the best poems arise from, is meant to be read: First one meaning, then another.

Changeling Lines

To men: You express love
but reserve doubt
and pandemonium results.

May 21, 1992
The previous poem, "Changing Lines," recast as a kind of haiku. As with that other poem, this also came to me.

Fireworks

Fourth of July approaches
And I go out, solitary
for a pleasure reserved
for group watching
But that is, in reality
a solitary pleasure
severally enjoyed.

June 20, 1992
Some pleasures are wonderful to enjoy with others, and yet the pleasure is inside each person alone.

Meeting of Minds

Two cholerics meet in space
Explode on contact
Face to face
Shouting, reddened, anger-driven
This the joy for which they've striven.

February 24, 1993
This poem makes more sense—and is far funnier—if you understand the four Hippocratic temperaments. For those who don't: speaking in general, cholerics aren't nice about the feelings of others, believe in the Law of the Jungle (where they are King or Queen) and the Survival of the Fittest (themselves). And they enjoy combat.

Pretending

Our bodies shape themselves
Out of moonlight and sorrow
Laying thick layers of flesh on thin
Until the illusion of invulnerability
Is complete.

March 11, 2001
Another stealth poem. I have no recollection of writing this, yet there it was in a journal in my own handwriting, written exactly as you see it here, with no scratchings-out or revisions, discovered in 2006, five years after the writing.

A Mother's Love

The blow that never comes
Or the blow that comes too swift
For thought or fear,
These things...

The heart that never yields
Walled high against the world
Compassion never felt,
These things...

The words that cut so deep
The weeping souls that flinch
But keep still their tongues in fear,
These things...

These things the body remembers
And long after only silence reigns
Where terror once ruled
Long after the silent ashes of holocaust have settled
Long after...

The body still quivers and takes no solace
Because the arms that should have comforted
The heart that should have bled
The voice that should have soothed
Were the weapons used

April 10, 2006

What happens to a woman's children when that woman is unfit to be a mother? When she lashes out irrationally at those she should be cherishing? When her very presence is a source of terror for her children? Have you ever seen a person with one shoulder slightly hunched, as though expecting a blow that never comes? What endlessly repeated abuse brought that to pass? And how can such an injured soul be healed?

Stories and storytellers

Storytellers have a long and honored role in the history of human society—their stories retain continuity, so we remember how things were, see how far we've come, how much we've changed—or haven't changed—and can understand our place in the grand sweep of human existence. Cognitive scientists have found that the human brain is wired to pay attention to stories. (Writers, take note: If you want to get your readers' attention, tell a story.) The poems in this chapter each tell a story.

White Stone Weekend

Magical days...

I.
The Storyteller speaks,
Weaves her craft.
She moves, turns head,
Touches gently
Hand to knee, then
The magic pulls
and we are in her story;
a tale always
of good and evil
though the names change.
When she finishes this installment
We return to find ourselves
Safe, on an orange couch
In the afternoon sun.

II.
The Wizard visits
His familiar, too,
Although disguised.
His cloak swirls
Though he is still.
Elementals roil the air
Obedient to his staff.
A careless word destroys them.

III.
A special one,
The Adventurer;
Nourishes unknown hurts.
His sword: keen wit
And deadly
Which belies his innocent mien.
A leather thong around his neck
Holds pieces of his journey—
Talismans of knowledge:
Star, eagle, broken jade scarab...
Name them easily.
His soul is more elusive.

Stories and storytellers

IV.
Return, no longer free:
Have I ever been
Since the phoenix rose before me
Entrancing in his brilliance?
I went when he beckoned—
Who would not?
But now I find molten chains
So flexible when hot
Bind too closely when cool.

May 3, 1977

Each person mentioned in this poem visited me over the course of one weekend. The "white stone" refers to Lewis Carroll's habit of marking good days in his journal as "white stone" days. The Storyteller and I are still friends after the long pull of years. The Wizard and his familiar, and the Adventurer, were all friends of friends, their names long lost in the dust of time. The Phoenix, my partner at the time, didn't like me to have friends..

One More River

Sad evening of leavetaking:
Cheerful smiles
Pensive looks when no one sees
Sad hearts where no one feels
Save each alone.
The lights aren't dim enough—
I can see the sorrow
And feel it.
Many here tonight
Feel
A tearing asunder
Of more than a well-loved friend
Already gone in his mind
(I saw you leave—in a dream—two nights ago).
Some security leaves with you
Of a well-established life
And power games
(Do you remember? We played with children—
Games of good and evil
And neutrals
But the time came for children to grow
And so we left them
Though some hardly knew our presence
and others felt us gods.)
There are some possibilities here
Never yet explored
Perhaps never will be.
Return would not be the same
As everyone knows
And most regret.
Though I must admit
My spirit's bent
Is independence too
And so I understand
Though startled by moon-messages.

Plans make reality
And lines of thought
Make the room alive
With light and dark

Stories and storytellers

Spiderwebs.
Attempts to entangle
And impede
And organize into permanent structures
Are constantly destroyed.
We all know the inevitable,
And say to what was
And never was
Farewell.

August 28, 1979

During my years at Santa Clara University and for a while after, I was on the periphery of a group of people—literate, fantastical, enamored with themselves. At a post-college going-away party for one of the members of this group, I had an intense sense that things were changing forever for everyone present. People were splitting apart, going to far-off places, diving, as it were, into the stream of life, being swept away, perhaps never to be seen again. I didn't know at the time that I was picking up on everyone's feelings; my awareness of my intuitive/empathic abilities came many years later. All I was aware of at the time was that the feelings I was experiencing were odd and strange and didn't feel comfortable in my skin, which I have since learned is a sure sign that they weren't my feelings.

Transformavit

The maiden lay, indolent,
asking for it,
sleepily in the sun.
Nearby, the corn was tended
and the tanned bodies of youths
premiered in her dreams.
Safe between her and them
a river murmured song. This,
and the distant chaff and laughter
of boys two steps from men
were the only sounds on that sun-drenched
slow afternoon. Nightmare enters:
Come to row's end, a boy-man spies maiden
And shouts, Here is fine game.
She, no fool as to feel that all dreams,
become reality, are desirable,
startles full awake, heart pounding.
More youths saunter up, not yet sure
what is expected of them.
The maiden knows, and decides for them
by giving herself to the river.
Father, mother, it embraces her, tries to hide her
from the dawning awareness in young men's eyes.
The race begins.
A strong swimmer, the nymph has the advantage
and gains a bend while the men doubt yet.
They shout, then, spirits up,
and something else, too, and pursue.
She comes to shallow rapids, and pants to her feet.
Normally fleet, they feel made of stone
and the once-helper water hinders her running.
Calls, commands behind her
indicate excited pursuit,
though the noise of water on rocks
heart sounding loudly
breath coming quickly
make it seem falsely distant.
She knows where she's going, though,
having discovered it when younger—
just yesterday—

and prays only to find it
with the lusty hunters still out of sight.
The sanctuary is gained
and proves to be a hole in a tree, hollowed by fire,
hidden by growth. The dryad turns,
scrambles up bank, squeezes into tree,
and tries to pant quietly.
Shouts come nearer. The fleetest,
knowing he will see her at last, doesn't.
The river flows subdued,
as though the gods have been at work,
in a straight course to the valley.
He slows, touched by awe and fear,
and knows
the river father has transformed his daughter
into a tree.

January 13, 1980

Written, based on a dream, while studying classical Latin and reading Ovid's Metamorphoses *in the original Latin. The poem's title means "changed" or "transformed." The shifts in tense in this poem are deliberate. My Latin teacher thought it was very classical Latin in feeling, which I had intended, and also thought that it was a very sexy poem, which I had not intended. Though I see his point now.*

Samurai

Your painted fierce face
Sleek black hair, banded in white,
Topknotted;
Embroidered silk kimono
White-green
Elaborately draped;
Tasseled sword;
Tasseled honor;
All these scowl, and the villagers back in awe.
But the children and the women
Samurai too
know.

September 1, 1980
The question to answer: What is it that the women and children know about the male samurai?

The Redeeming Factor

I.

There always is one.
Try to find it though
When your heart turns against you,
and nothing seems worth the pain.

II.

You can live through it
Just barely
And with lots of help.
If I really thought this would last forever
I wouldn't.

III.

The struggle this time:
To love oneself without conditions.

IV.

There was a woman once
Whose only criteria for everything
was that it be perfect:
Complete, finished, nothing could add.
And when she accepted at last that nothing ever could be
Even herself
Especially herself;
As she watched the cloud castles collapse
In a stately slow-motion dance
That was a process of perfection
(Though she didn't notice)
In itself,
She realized bitterly
That even a perfect suicide
Is impossible.

And besides, she'd have to come back
And do it all again.

Being a pragmatist,
she changed her definition
of perfection.

October 14, 1987
I wrote this poem during a desperately hard time in my life. Back then, nobody talked about postpartum depression, which is real and deadly. A single mother, I struggled with it alone. Two things saved me: Knowing that I was solely responsible for a precious new human being's life, and, when that failed one time, three angels sitting on me in the night to keep me from harming myself. I could feel them, but couldn't see them.

Stories and storytellers

Talking to myself

Rich gold
Gifts from within
frilly lace
on a smooth satin package.
Is it a girl?

An unknown
coming into my world.

Hey! Am I scared?
I am spinning on my toes
Not out of control
But dancing into a new place.

December 2, 1988

I wrote this poem when I received a sudden psychic impression that a co-worker was pregnant. I found out later she was. I never shared this with her, though, for two reasons: she wasn't a friend, and at the time I didn't talk about my psychic abilities

Time Travelers

We do it slowly, surely
One day at a time
Jailed for some crime
Someone says we committed.
I make no excuses here
But society is wrong
To regiment us so
And keep us away from it.
We miss so much
And learn so little.

When we emerge
Five years later, ten, twelve
The world has turned
Too many times for us.
"Maybe I'll rob a bank
Just this once
To tide me over"
To make me feel more comfortable
More familiar in an unfamiliar world
One of us said.
He had a job to go to
In two weeks
But no easy way to travel
from now to then
No money
No security
No paid-for roof over his head.

Now he's back inside
In the time machine.

December 3, 1991
I wrote this poem after reading an article by someone fresh out of prison who told of how difficult it was to make the transition from prison life to life outside, and of how some don't make it, and end up returning to the world they know, unable to operate in the world they feel themselves to be strangers within. It occurred to me then that being in prison must be like being in a one-way time machine.

Xanthippe

And wouldn't you be a bit crabby
Wouldn't you nag a little
If your husband was known as the gadfly
of the Senate?
Perhaps not in these days,
when the Senate could use a good gadfly.
But then—!
Yes, then, a man who takes pride
In annoying others
"For the sake of truth"
Could have done it more gently
And far more wisely
Couldn't he?
So he must have enjoyed his role
And certainly must have practiced at home
Wringing every last bit of the joy of the hunt
out of his words.
Parsimonious with his softness
Generous with the bile
Poking, biting, jabbing—
Until she could stand no more
And bit back

October 8, 1992

Xanthippe was Socrates' wife, who was supposed to be a bit of a nag. If you get to know me really really well, I'll explain this poem.

The Statue

Imagine this:
A statue of a man
Standing
Smiling easily
But with a glint in the eye.

Keep your mind on that glint.

A woman, glancing light from afar
Intrigued, attracted, approaches.

As she nears, the statue changes
Comes horribly to life
Subtly at first
Then drastically
Opening shaggy forearms
Fingers shaping into envenomed claws
Smile widening into a maw
Sharp teeth showing.
It waits.

Beglamoured by the image,
She misses the reality,
And stumbles forth into the waiting trap.
The beast attacks
Tearing, ripping, clawing;
Gone, all trace of man.

The shock awakens her.

Struggling, stunned, stalwart,
Fighting for her soul,
The poison makes her sluggish
Slows her beating heart
Turns feelings to stone.

Despairing, desperate, deliberate,
She wrenches herself away
Leaving stone and flesh in the razor claws.
Able only to crawl

Stories and storytellers

Bleeding and exhausted
To a safe distance.

She rests, then turns, and sees
A statue of a man
Smiling easily
A glint in the eye
Standing alone.

November 4, 1996
Sometimes things are not what they seem. Too many of us value outward appearance over inward substance

Cassandra

She was once a prophet
Singing the syllables of joy and alarm.
The symbols shaped themselves inside her
Until she had to express them
Unmistakable, unshakable.

One slip and the long fall from grace begins
Until nothing is certain anymore.
Prey to uncertainty, fear, and doubt
Aspersions cast within, without
Outside reflecting what was within
Until she saw the magic, felt it move within
And begin again.

October 5, 1998
Cassandra was doomed by Apollo to always foresee the future accurately, but to never be listened to. Before you say Apollo was an ass, hear the whole story: he wanted her, but she demanded the gift of prophecy before she would yield. He gave her the gift, but she refused him anyway, which is when he cursed her. Eventually Cassandra ended up as a slave to King Menelaus. When Menelaus returned home from the Trojan wars with Cassandra in tow, she warned him against going inside his home. He ignored he. His adulterous wife and her lover murdered both Menelaus and Cassandra. RIP.

Poems for my children

I never thought I'd write children's poetry. And I'd always felt a bit abashed that I've written a few less serious poems, including these few children's poems, as though a "real" poet didn't write anything light or frivolous. (James Thurber aside.) But then I discovered that many "serious" poets, including John Ciardi, whose translation of Dante's **Divine Comedy** is, well, divine, have written children's poems.

With these poems, I didn't intend to write a children's poem. I wrote "Second Story Cat," for example, when I was barely out of childhood myself and was gradually discovering what I had missed.

As I learned to honor and nurture that child in me who felt she never really got a chance to play the first time around, I started to write more poetry for her—and for my own daughter. Though I never wrote many poems specifically for children, because children are capable of far more than we give them credit for; "regular," "grown-up" poetry often speaks just as clearly, if not more clearly, to a child as children's poetry does.

Second Story Cat

Yes, I'm stuck here
A T.S. Eliot kind of cat—
Strictly high class,
And with a *most* interesting tale—
Though I'll never have a chance to tell it.
Born, raised—I'll probably die here,
Disgusting fact.
One story up from all those glorious smells—
Other cats, rats, maybe even a dragon or two—
(For me to tame, you know).

Mom can go out
Prowl and return
But I can only sit on this landing
Closely guarded, I might add
And quickly brought in.
Five months old and the world is still a mystery to me.
I'm fierce and fast—
No dog could get me!
And curious
But no soap.
I'm still a kitten to *her*.

I'd run away, but I'm not allowed down the stairs.

June 6, 1977
I had a cat who was not allowed outside, but could come out on a balcony. It seemed to bother him that he could not go further. Of course, the "mom" is me, not his feline mom.

The Smiling Bear

If you should ever meet a bear
Smiling in his underwear
Watch out! For who knows who or where
He got them from.

No, no, mistake me not, it's just
That bears who smile are rarely fussed
About such niceties as "please"
And "thank you" when acquiring these.

For bears won't wear just anything
And some bears can't help noticing
That people's clothes will suit them fine—
I just don't want to give them mine.

So smiling bears upon the earth
Are good—just give them a wide berth
And skip along another path
To so avoid a bare bear's wrath.

July 21, 1992
Just for fun. Mostly. Watch out for bears.

Why Snakes Should Not Wear Ties

Snakes and ties just don't agree
Listen, children, and you'll see
Why long thin snakes and long thin ties
Belong together like truth and lies
Which is to say they should never
Ever think of going together.

There was a snake of mild demeanor
Whose cousin snake could not be meaner
The cousin snake was always teasing
The mild snake into acts displeasing
Making him do things quite ridiculous
Such as reciting poetry meticulous
And boring in front of fifth-grade snakes
Who'd boo and hiss and brandish rakes
(A sign of disrespect to snakes)
Until he'd quietly slip away
A sadder snake.

The cousin once roped him into wearing
A tie of gold with small red herring
decorations down the side
And front to greet his unmet bride.

It was a source of merriment
Among the townsnakes's government.

The day the she-snake came to town
A mail-order bride for this snake clown
She took one look at her poor groom
Declared she'd sooner marry a broom
And rode out again on the next stage.
Leaving a snake stricken with rage
Against his cousin snake who'd cozened
him into being something he wasn't.
He tore off the tie and followed after
His beautiful bride thin as a rafter.

Poems for my children

It gladdens all to hear the ending
Was happily not at all heart-rending;
Instead the two snakes married fondly
And had three small snakes—Gay, Bright, and Frondly
Who obey their parent's call and beck.

The tie? It's on the cousin's neck.

July 21, 1992
Another "just for fun" poem.

Friends, family, and lovers

My romantic relationship poems are about men. (I'm a cis-gendered women whose preferred pronouns are she/her.) Other poems in this chapter are about people I loved as friends. A few are about family.

I say this next part not to get pity, because I don't need it, but to let others know they aren't alone and that there's no shame in making bad choices. I'm tempted to add, "as long as you learn from them," but with deep wounds it can take years, decades, a lifetime to learn what our choices are telling us about ourselves.

For much of my life, I chose unworthy and sometimes abusive lovers and friends; people who were acting out of their own wounds and generational trauma, people who showed me, as unmistakably as they could, that the qualities I so admired and thought, in my idealistic naivety, I saw in them, were mine instead. These actions on my part were a fine demonstration of Jungian shadow projection. (Few people outside serious Jungian scholars know this: Carl Jung wrote that our shadows can also be good things about ourselves that we deny are true.)

I attributed those admirable qualities to people I loved because I couldn't attribute them to myself.

I was disastrously bad at discriminating between what people said about themselves and what they actually did, and my poetry shows it. We expect of others what we are ourselves. Honest to a fault, I always believed the words people spoke. It just never occurred to me that some people lie as a matter of course. I was always shocked, disappointed, and eventually angered when I was betrayed. Until I finally, finally realized the profound truth in two sayings: Actions speak louder than words, and, as Maya Angelou said, "when someone shows you who they are, believe them the first time."

I'm still an idealist and I think now that I always will be (the difference being, really, that I am more comfortable with it), but I've learned to look at relationships with a more balanced eye and with more realistic expectations for both the other and myself. And to pay more attention to actions rather than to words. And, I might add, to value myself more highly, so that I now experience a much different sort of person in my life.

Because I've grown and healed, I've been tempted to just throw out all those old love poems—those old reminders of who I was—just as I've let go of my old ideas about myself. I was and still am embarrassed by those love poems because I allowed myself to idealize people, and I feel I'm at fault for my misjudgments. It never occurred to me to think that maybe, just maybe, the abusive person is the one who should be embarassed and ashamed of themselves. But that's not going to happen: If they were capable of that much self-awareness and self-honesty, not to mention empathy and compassion, they wouldn't be abusive.

However, out of a sense of honesty; and also respect for my younger self's strength and integrity and honesty and even, yes, innocence; and a grudging admission that though the subjects were poorly chosen, some of those poems are decent poems; I've restrained myself from tossing out the embarrassing poems. Some poems didn't survive the various purges; I long ago deleted most of my early poems because they were just too cringeworthy.

We make our own happiness, but it takes two to make a joyful relationship.

Love's Labor Lost

I fell into a pit
And the falling took so long
The days turned into months
The dark my only dawn.
I wept in utmost pain
Lamenting Love's defeat
I fell into a pit
But landed on my feet.

June 2, 1976

I believe Emily Dickinson gave me this poem in spirit. My reasons for saying that: The poem came to me complete, with no composition or editing on my part; it is very much in her style, which is not much like my style; it felt like a message to me about something that I would eventually experience, not about something that I had already experienced; it is a far better poem than the general sort I was writing at the time. Of course, there is no way of proving whether I got this from Emily or simply had an instant of creativity that was beyond my everyday capabilities at the time.

Storm

You
Almost had me hooked
But I slipped away
Tearing flesh and trailing heavy sinkers of despair
Into the cool clear waters of freedom.

1976

This is what remains of a three-page poem I wrote at the end of a painful relationship. After I wrote it, I showed it to Jim Torrens, SJ, a known and respected poet, one of my honored instructors at Santa Clara University, and a friend. Jim had often said I had "it," by which he meant a gift for poetry. About this poem's original form, he said most of what I had written was too specifically personal and wouldn't appeal to anyone else. So I trimmed the three pages to these five lines. It was hard to part from both the relationship and the anguished long poem, but essential. In writing, "kill your darlings" doesn't mean kill your favorite characters; it means delete anything you've written that doesn't serve the story. This poem was published in the winter 1976 issue of Santa Clara University's student literary journal, The Owl.

Friends, family, and lovers

Shadow

She steals her own happiness
Pulverizes it between the pestle of Pride
And the mortar of Despair
Then loudly laments the loss
While holding tightly to the unhappiness she so carefully shaped
From her tears
Mixed with the powder of joy.

January 8, 1978

Written about a friend who created the problems she complained about, and seemed to take a perverse pleasure in them. I once incautiously compared her with Eeyore, about which she was enormously offended. Decades later, mentioning this fact to her sister, I learned her family also called her Eeyore.

A.J.M.

He's good with things electrical
He keeps them all symmetrical
With measurings quite metrical
And chosen flows (select trickle).

May 1978
For some reason, AJM, an electrical engineer, hated this poem.

Friends, family, and lovers

Silence in the Tropics

Back to closed doors
I find silence
In uneasy company
Heavier than aloneness.
Violence in our hearts
World views poles apart
Screened by fans of courtesy.
Palm fronds mask ice
Snow veils torrid zones
So likenesses melt when at last
Surmising gaze sees through flesh false
To alien bones.

November 30, 1979
A roommate was unconscious of, and therefore acting out, their own generational trauma. When two people are still in denial about their generational trauma, communication fails.

Moon Song

I rode on a river of clouds last night
The moon was howling high
My caution was down and my spirits up
As I silvered through the dark sky.

The river of clouds was flowing fast
Though sandbars blocked the way
I sped along—the pull was strong
For I was feeling fey.

The moon lit my course at first full well
So all was clear to see
Below I saw plains of faery folk
And some acknowledged me.

Their actions were clear though the meanings not
A dance to the death, it seemed
Intricate, careful, yet painfully rough
My straight course was better, I deemed.

Further I sped, and soon came above
A valley ill-lit by the moon
A blackness welled thick from its ill-formed walls
Its sorcerer caused me to swoon.

The power of love is a subtle thing
And friendship much stronger than hate
How I escaped I cannot tell
But I think love of friends and of Fate.

My journey continues—it may never end
Though well past that ill valley am I
With friends and love and my own strong will
I continue to roam the bright sky.

December 8, 1979
This poem came to me in one quick flow.

Friends, family, and lovers

Summer Honey (for James Torrens, SJ)

In twenty-one days they drop
Having worked themselves dead
For their hive, for their queen.
No wonder, then, that they
Wax angry, dive dizzily
At my head, helmeted,
And spacesuit-garbed body,
When I, alien giantess,
Rob their hive of its sweetness.
How can they know that I
With an eye to future
Thefts, leave them enough
And more, to survive?
They can't. And yet they do.

So to you, most dear friend
I send gentle reminder:
The result of your work
Is a honey that none
Can steal. The remainder
Of the moral is yours
To divine as you see fit.

December 9, 1979

James Torrens, SJ, was a professor at Santa Clara University when I was attending. He was a respected poet, and invited me to an invitation-only poetry class. When I shyly showed him a few of my poems, he said I definitely had the gift, but could work on making my poems less personal. Okay, though I feel that all my poems are intensely personal. I wrote this poem for and about him (I kept bees at the time), calligraphed it on parchment, and framed it as a gift for him. I never knew what he thought of the youthful presumptuousness of my writing this poem, let alone giving it to him.

Mirror

Aye, that's all I was
Though you denied it
Claiming instead to see clearly—
As through glass—
To my very core.
And the devils you saw there!
Writhing in flame dances
Attractive to your gentle moth soul
(The one you pinned and mounted carefully
To keep from stain or ruin)
Despite yourself.
Clear sighted?
I never saw one so blind and afraid,
And so happy with his own pinning.

September 26, 1980
Projection and denial—a powerful one-two punch.

Friends, family, and lovers

Galahad the Unchanging

I.

In some other place you ride
Forever bold, forever the brave knight
Riding rescue.
But not here, not in this time
Though pieces of that other world
Slip to us through the gaps in ours, Gallereth.
Hence your name. Hence my occasional surrender
Though I am honed steel, fit for my own battles,
Not some tapestry-weaving maiden
Bemused by unicorns.

II.

That strange bloody beast.
Our history
Has virgins luring unicorns to their deaths.
This ancient perfidy
Has been twisted into glory by our times.
I know of some whose mired eyes
Betray themselves, as their needle-bright tongues,
Stitch-stitching through conversations and time
Betray others to the killing sword.
I understand their fascination with unicorns.
It is a thing very much of this world.

III.

And knights?
The swords were theirs that cut the trusting necks.
It was their duty. Or maybe sport.
But I, no maiden, yet tender-hearted still
Cherish things of magic. I will not kill
By allowing the rough steel of your reality
To cut what, in the end, is me
Being mine.
That would be the ultimate betrayal,
One that I would not survive.

IV.

In some other place you ride
My silken scarf tied to your side. But here—
I feel and sing the world's gaps
You live by stern solidity.
Yet you feel that armor shining heavy on your breast,
And seek to rescue me
From myself.

Dear Knight!
Out of duty,
You would destroy the very thing you love.

October 21, 1980
Galahad Gallereth was my private name for my lover at the time. This poem includes references to friends of his as well. It was a bit unnerving, decades later, to find out that the person with the needle-bright tongue had taken up embroidery, a thing she would have scorned when I wrote this poem. I make no claims for prescience, but the connection is there nonetheless.

Sorcerer

Preparations carefully done
He speaks the word aloud.
Surprise! No ordin Ariel
But starry maiden wrapped in clouds
Of planets and chill galaxies.
Beyond his hopes this wonder is
(The crocodile smiles)
But not beyond his dreams: This Wiz
Has wanted her awhile.
Their universes then combine
Unlooked-for consummation
But sparks will always fly from the
Resulting conflagration.

December 10, 1980

Inspired by seeing a greeting card (by the artist Michael Hague, I believe) with a wizard conjuring a maiden and being surprised by her appearance. A stuffed crocodile hangs in the wizardly workshop (which is crowded with magical paraphernalia). In the picture, you can tell that the maiden and the wizard do not belong in each other's worlds. Ariel is a reference to the spirit in Shakespeare's The Tempest, *and not to the famous mermaid who came long after I wrote this poem.*

Sorceress-Shapechanger

The Leopard's claws and tawny spotted hide
And languid leaning powerful repose,
The Lynx's tufted ears and velvet glide
When choosing shapes at will these you disclose.
While human, you do jeweled daggers wear,
And 'broidered gowns, and capes that sweep the ground
Withal, you stalk about with regal stare
Yet still sometimes your eyes show you feel bound.
But in the background, rearing golden-chained,
Desiring freedom from too-binding ties,
The Unicorn, so stunning, silver-maned,
Shakes loose her chains, and with the wind she flies.
> Her shape is yours, more so than all the rest;
> With joy of it, and life, may you be blessed.

December 10, 1980
Written for a woman who thought little of herself. I saw more and hoped to encourage her. She hated this poem. In retrospect, and understanding a bit more about self-esteem, I understand that some people focus on their negatives even when you compliment them.

Friends, family, and lovers

Fool's Gold

What is of worth, then, to you?
The proven gold at hand
Is spurned for the distant flash
That gleams and keeps its distance,
Aware that close scrutiny
Reveals true worth.

The wise one knows
That the true gold is this:
What is offered freely
Is not always worthless,
Nor easy.
Nor is the hard-to-obtain
Often more than a costly mistake.
Take care; think twice:
Gold unrecognized
Is easily lost.

January 26, 1981
People so often judge the worth of something by how hard it is to obtain. This can be a mistake.

Leavetaking

Well, Father
You had your own life to live, to be sure
And I mine. But did you think
Of the scars?

A child's mind
Is quite literal. One only abandons
What is of no use
Or has lost its worth.
But that mind also
Buries things easily.
Tomorrow is eons off
Yesterday is ancient, pre-Cambrian stuff
Metamorphosed under the weight
Of today, whose urgency is strengthened thus.

Did I cry then? I don't remember,
But the festering wound of abandonment
Became so permanent
That I didn't know life could be without it.

All this life has been a contradiction:
Things happened easily, or never;
Life was marvelous, or I could never win.
And it all goes back to a child
Whose magic life was disenchanted
So that traces of the golden touch remained
But lead weighted every step thereafter.

My heart cries now for all the years:
For years of dreaming that the day would come
When you would claim me, pull clouds from the sun
And shower gold upon me once again
That sunny gold of life and renewed love.

And now—
You chose your life, and I do now choose mine:
To lose that leaden weight, unburden heart,
And live the golden life now free from pain.

Friends, family, and lovers

Revised June 29, 1982

My biological father abandoned the family when I was 6 or 7. Fortunately, I had a wonderful stepfather from 7 to 15. He and I lost touch of each other, then reunited joyfully 50 years later. My biological father's abandonment scarred me emotionally. I wrote this poem when I was beginning to realize just how much harm is done when a father abandons his children.

Heart's Sister (for Kathe)

Winter's Child
With the look of spring in your eyes.
Shoulders hunched (for now)
Against the cold.
Always the daffodils bloom again
Profligate with their yellow wealth
Shocking the timid
Delighting the bold
Including (of course) Winter's last children
Whose task, after all, is this:
To thaw hard knowledge
Thaw solid winter
Thaw hearts
And let loose the floods of love.

February 7, 1981
"Winter's last children" are Aquarians. Kathe's and my mothers had been friends since late elementary school, when my mother's family had taken Kathe's mother under their wings as almost another daughter. Our mothers remained friends until my mother's death. I never knew the full story of what was going on in Kathe's mother's home that she needed a safe haven at my mother's home.

Friends, family, and lovers

False Dawn

And did I look for gold, and find but dross?
And did I feel my hopes, alas, were vain?
And was my story but of love and loss?
Yet was I tempered by this early pain.
My heart is hammered gold, all dross removed
Through trial of ice and fire I've won my name
'Til now at last I feel my heart's been proved:
The core and essence still remain the same.
This, then, is how our love has come to be
Not accident or fate, but tearful quest
Through dark of soul and out again to see
Your smile, and know my worth: naught but the best.
    Your worth to me is all that's come before
    For it has brought me safely to your door.

April 1981
Dross after all. Don't ask about what he did to the ducks.

Touch of Kings

Welsh magic woven silver in your hair
Compassion's touches tender on your face
The hands of kings so sturdy and so fair
Bespeak the mystic heritage of your race.
Unspoken words leap clearly from your eyes
Which shift with moods from steely grey to blue
Unsteadying my heart, which was so wise
To know you first, and lead me home to you.
Your wisdom and your grace both keep apace
With how you love me—gently and so fair,
Expanding joyful love which knows no trace
Of seeking traps where no such thing is there.
    Unequaled man, your loving queen am I
    And full of heart—a richness I can't buy.

June 10, 1982
Another step on my journey home: idealization of the other, denial of my own worth, and projection.

Light and Shadow

A slender book
Covered in black velvet
Silver unicorn imprinted on the front:
Paradoxes. Velvet softens
The black, a dramatic color
Worn by people who ought to wear cloaks
And silk-sheathed daggers, always.
The color, some say, of evil,
If evil existed, or of night, negation, death.
And the Unicorn, a symbol of purity
Of hope, of purpose, of life itself
Singing joy in every cell.
A unicorn, a slender book, black velvet.
I thought of you.

July 8, 1982

I wrote this poem when giving a slim, velvet-covered journal with a unicorn stamped on the front cover to the same person for whom I wrote "Sorceress-Shapechanger" on page 110. Because I admired her, the message I wanted to convey was that she was an interesting woman. I meant this poem to be a compliment. It wasn't received that way.

Possessions

We have a computer
And a lot of love

An oak table
Built solidly, to last the years of our lives.

Two golden-eyed cats, like negatives of each other
White and black.

Thunderstorms, and their wild energy
Purple lightning, and hard rain

Ideas breathed in
With the air around us, and out again

And a few good friends we'd die for
Were dying required, and not life

July 8, 1982
Note to future editors: the lack of a period at the end of this poem is deliberate.

Friends, family, and lovers

Soul Poisoner

Your slow venom
Eats to the heart drop by drop
Acidly etching your lies and hate
Into an innocent love.

September 20, 1982
As the character Wash says in the television show Firefly, *"Curse your sudden but inevitable betrayal!"*

Good-bye, Adventurer

I expected kinder treatment
From a man whose history tells
Of a heart too hurt to live.

Guess I misread the clues;
Must've pushed a few wrong buttons:
I got the acid and an early end
To the game.

April 12, 1984
When I wrote this poem, a game based on The Hitchhiker's Guide to the Galaxy *had recently been released. In the game, pushing the wrong buttons brought about an unexpected and fatal acid bath.*

Friends, family, and lovers

Shining Sun

Looking up
In happy astonishment

A year's long distance
Has brought no unwelcome silences.
Instead, the love flows so strong
I swim in warmth for hours.

And somewhere his feet
Touched a golden path of sureness
As strangely and inexorably as mine
So that we are now at
perfect ease; we
Recognize, rejoice in
A whole being, come home.

Shining Sun,
Winter here, summer here
In my heart forever.
We are one.

November 11, 1984
For my brother David, whom I hadn't seen in a year.

The Trap

Silent hawk
Wings tilting, shining
in the sun
In the heat
Eyes alert for the least movement
of the cat below.
She scurries
Leaps, plays, hides among the rocks
And thorny cactus
Unaware.
Her world is the earth,
not the air.

A shadow passes.

The cat looks up, startled.
And before she can move
The hawk's talons
Pierce her heart.

December 7, 1984
I used to make a lot of bad choices when it came to men.

Clear Water

Like water, you move
Change
Run swiftly over still stones
Stand deeply in the desert sun
Fall gently through the waiting air
To fall upon your mother earth
And nourish her.
And like water
You are shaped by what surrounds you
Imprisoned by the outside
Because you have no shape of your own.

October 7 & 14, 1987
It's impossible to have a rational conversation with irrational people.

Shattered Mirrors

You never liked what you saw
Hated it, in fact
In those mirrors.
So you took the direct route
The short way
The quick approach:
A fist through the mirror's heart.
Unfortunately
(And maybe you guessed this)
There's a trick to mirrors
And it was your own heart
Consumed
Still being consumed
In those long-ago flames
Whose pain, destroying you,
You tried to stop.

October 14, 1987
In the process of projection, we deny that something is true about ourselves, then project it out onto one or more people (that is, we see it in others) so we can criticize them for being what we actually are. The best way to get out of projection and denial is to recognize that you are looking in a mirror, not at someone else—that what you see in others is at least in part a reflection of something—some belief about yourself, perhaps—that you have sent out onto someone else to view more clearly.

Friends, family, and lovers

To a Little Green Snake in the Grass

I have such a literal mind.
I took the beauty of your form
For what you really are
Until you bit my ankle once too often
Then I felt your quick clever poison.

February 20, 1989
Written for someone who pretended to be a friend. I didn't see through her until she incautiously attributed to me things I would never have thought about her, let alone said. A lot of mysterious actions suddenly made sense as I realized that projection and denial were once again having their way with someone,

The Fire at Midnight

Owl brother
Wise and silent
Wings spread on the dark night wind
on the cool night winds
You slide through the air
on fire.

How could you not know
soul secrets?

Here's one for you:
You are one with the night wind
One with the fire
And one with love.

June 16, 1989
For my brother Peter.

Refreshment

Sweet water after alkali
A cool river of air in the hot desert night
Gentle hands after scourging whips
A tangy nectarine on parched lips
Substance, not smoke
Fire and air
A keen mind and reflective eye.
We talk in silence.
Terra cognito, firm and sure underfoot
And the vast silky sky before us.

July 14, 1989

Waiting for Him

Waiting for him
It seems I've spent a lifetime doing it.
At restaurants
      In the car
            Picking him up from work
And waiting for him to listen
To hear me
To understand.

November 1992
Of course, waiting for someone can also mean "waiting for the right person to come along," though that isn't what I had in mind when I wrote this.

Friends, family, and lovers

The Ten of Swords Looks for the Easy Out

Were I to play Guinevere
To your King Arthur—
Allow the timeless story
of indifference, passion, and betrayal
To wash over me—
Were I to allow you that choice of endings
It would be a betrayal worse than any physical
A wound deeper than words
And I, not you, the victim of deceit.

June 13, 1993

The Tarot card Ten of Swords signifies betrayal. This poem came to me after a fierce months-long struggle in my heart to forgive someone who had injured me a great deal over many years. The hardest part was finding the willingness to forgive him. When I finally granted that willingness, the struggle ended, and a miracle happened: A celestial love poured through my heart. That outpouring of love lasted five months. During that period, I realized many things, including that much of what I had assumed was true because that man had said it with his lips turned out to be the opposite when I looked into his heart. Yet it didn't matter. When you have that intense love pouring through you, it is easier, not harder, to see the truth about people, even when that truth is what some might call unpleasant. The thing is, in that flow of love, you no longer desire to judge it. You just See it. The same person apologized to me ca. 2002 about a fundamental lie he'd been telling for years, and in doing so, confirmed what I had long suspected.

Wrapped in arms

Wrapped in arms of strength and comfort
Drifting in and out of sleep
Knowing self and other deeply
Loved, throughout eternity
Thus it is to know contentment
Thus it is to be complete.

Thus I sing of love forever
When clean the winds of time do sweep
All other ties to earth and fortune
Out among the ocean deep.

December 1998
Written while thinking one day how nice it would be to have a man hold me and I could feel that he loved me. So, written for a future lover, and not anyone in my life at the time.

Friends, family, and lovers

Relationships

Understanding mirror images
Resignation and disgust
Hickory knows how to barbecue.
Some treat it like a game
Others seek solitude
Eternally pouncing on the single lone article the.

July 12, 2000
Another poem that came to me, this one unusual in that it came to me last line first, which may have something to do with the reference to mirror images. I can't say yet that I have figured this one out, and the third line sounds like complete nonsense, but it resists removal: The poem just doesn't feel right when I delete it.

Long she wept by the sea

long she wept by the sea
Or, wandering among the redwoods,
Those tall giants whose roots
Have gripped the earth and drunk deep from the soil
Since times long past, she reflected on happier times
And remembered long walks among the red trunks.
"These," she mused, "Have endured much, withstood storms
And drought, and so shall I,"
And with that she fell silent,
her grief now too deep for words.

June 11, 2014
I had just been told that a ten-year relationship, my first good one ever, was ending in just 13 days. It was a shock and a surprise. When I wrote this, I was reading Ovid's Metamorphoses, *in translation this time, not in the original Latin. (For a poem written when I was studying classical Latin and translating Ovid from the original, see "Transformavit" on page 80.) So this poem, which came to me whole and complete in an instant, is influenced by the classical Latin style. The lowercase at the start is deliberate, to give the feeling that you've dropped into the poem midway, and that there is more before. Which there is; I just didn't get to my notebook fast enough.*

The Ghosts of Never

Context is everything
That "no" sank me,
A lost ship of treasure.

And now my heart—
Barnacled, stove-to, submerged,
Its measure known only
To strange sea creatures
Who explore my depths,
Curious, unconcerned,
And to the ghosts of never—
Has suffered a sea change.

Take a long breath
A pause to reflect
A moment of calm
That isn't as dire as it sounds.

Tides change, oak rots, steel rusts
But my strength does not
And love changed in form
Is love still.

If lover is out of the question
I'll take shipmate with joy.

July 3, 2017

No means no. I wish I'd known, when I wrote this poem, about Chaucer's famous line from his Canterbury Tales, *"if gold rusts, what then can iron do?" I would have worked that in to the part where I say "Tides change, oak rots, steel rusts/but my strength does not."*

Cycles and circles

Most of my poems stand alone. But some I wrote as a series, exploring a theme from different angles, with different poetic sounds. Sometimes this just means two poems, paired; other times it means more. This chapter holds most of those poems. (In other chapters, you'll find a few poems related to each other.)

Many of these are love poems. I sigh when I read them. I started each relationship with so much hope and idealism, but I chose so badly—oh, so very badly—in the past. I like to think that I've now learned enough and healed enough to discern more clearly between the image and the substance, for I still feel believe that true, deep, sustaining love can exist and last.

Phoenix Rising

Glamorous
He glitters before you
And beckons.
His fire dazzles;
Deft illusions replace reality.
Everything shifts
Changes;
Confusions crowd your mind
And nothing is the same
Nothing.
Balance lost, you clutch him for support,
But fall, like Alice,
Fading through a mirror.

Bright colors whirl
Rapidly changing
Spinning
Nausea.
You land, but you are lost
Left with a handful of bright feathers
That burn.

June 24, 1977
This is the first poem in my Phoenix cycle. The reborn phoenix is a higher expression of the sign of Scorpio. The lower expression is the vengeful scorpion. In my optimistic way, I wanted to see this man expressing his phoenix instead of his scorpion. Although he told many stories of his childhood, most of them heart-rending, I didn't understand he was suffering from generational trauma because I had never heard the term back then. Nobody had.

Phoenix Flies

Good-bye.
You're off again
Soaring above our heads.
The cats blink
They've seen it before
And dangle paws off perch
Only in hope of catching the feather
That dances sideways
Glittery-gold
(How bright it seems in your reflected glare)
From the hot wind of your flight.

What they don't know is that I
The fourth cat on the scene
A Blue Cat, no longer ordinary
(You saw to that)
Am bored with this show—
I've seen it before too, you see—
And will be gone
By the time you return.

June 24, 1977

Another in the Phoenix cycle. The Blue Cat refers to the cat hero in Catherine Cate Coblentz's The Blue Cat of Castletown *(Longman's, Green and Co., Inc., 1949). The blue cat's destiny was to not be ordinary, but only if certain circumstances happened. He fulfilled his destiny by barely escaping a greedy, grasping man who wanted to destroy him. If you haven't read the book, I recommend it.*

Love Dawns

When dawning grey broke through the midnight black
Lost sleep was not missed overmuch by thee
T'was then I found what for so long was lack
Though awkward shy, you took my hint and me.
My love, you held me gentler than the night
So capturing all—hands, mind, and (later) heart
And all is passing great when it is right
Your love allowing me to take my part.
You feared at first, as do I still betimes
Yet still you took, and gave, all that you could
In trusting me you showed me that new times
Demand new roles, if loving will be good.
    My Lord, you name me Sorceress. I name you
    Wizard, Keeper of Hearts, and my love true.

June 13, 1978
This sonnet is the first in a cycle of five poems. I wrote the first four in fifteen minutes while on break while working as a librarian in the San Jose Mercury News' morgue. Like most of my poems, there were no errors, no erasures, no rewrites—the four came to me entire, and it was up to me to write them down as fast as I could. I received the fifth poem in the series a few days later. With such poems, there's an aspect of translation, as though I'm hearing the poem in another language, and I'm translating it into English. The man this poem series is about has a sterling character and is still a friend, lo these many years later. We were even married for seven years. We just weren't suited for each other.

The Past Is Released

Why should I say my loves have done me wrong?
All that is past. Behold! What now there be
For mine to hold—thy love so warming strong,
And naught the world offers matches thee.
I once despaired of ever half so much
And calmly, sadly, settled for none less
I hoped, but knew there couldn't be one such
As thee. That was my thought, to my distress.
Yet see! My hopes are overmatched by thee
Your strength and warmth and poet's heart heal mine
I do you wrong to carp of past debris
I'll put that all aside. My future's thine.
    In need of soothing old hurts, I may slide.
    But know thou this: I do not you deride.

June 13, 1978

The second sonnet in the cycle of five poems. The first few lines refer to my belief that it's never a good idea to dwell on past relationships when entering a new one.

Hope Is Renewed

Thy wonder grows, not bates, as once I feared
And mine, as eager, matches pace for pace
Though slow at first because in hurt immured
I quickly came to find joy in thy face.
All else but love, you say, takes second place
And this I say for me is also true
Why then, how can we but the sun outpace
By finding at day's end our love anew?

June 13, 1978
The third poem in the cycle of five. It isn't a sonnet as the other four are. I wrote down what came to me. I might have been interrupted, though interruptions are rare in a newspaper's lonely morgue.

Magical Salmon

My love, how can I tell what joy does leap
As fish from stream in rainbow energy
At sight of you, and knowledge that I keep
You, loving, wise, and free so close to me?
True hearts are we, and lucky to have found
So early in life's path our matching beat
You know my thoughts though I have made no sound
What need of other proof that our minds meet?
Once others taught us both to least expect
Two loving hearts as generous as we
How can we hurt where we need to protect
A treasured love that melds two such as we?
    So plight I, love, though shyly, troth to thee
    And hope you can so great return to me.

June 13, 2078

The fourth poem in the cycle of five. The magical salmon of the title refers to the salmon in the Welsh tale, "Culhwch and Olwen."

00: The Wizard's Cast

Wizard, your spell is cast, your roll is won
Did ever Sorceress have better luck?
Your gamble paid aye well not just for one
Two hearts from dire stake true love did pluck.
I tell you now I thought at first t'was me
And only me who cast the spell so tight
It wasn't long before I came to see
Your Wizard's spell, though subtle, had great might.
So now we hold each other in our hearts
And dare who will our sturdy tower storm
They'll find that we so loving do our parts
To nourish this deep love, and further form.
    I tell you now, Wizard, full glad am I
    That me you chose to love, and not pass by.

June 20, 1978
This final sonnet in the cycle of five poems came to me a few days afer I wrote the first four. Zero zero (00; pronounced "aught aught") refers to a face on a twenty-sided die used in a game called Dungeons and Dragons. *Rolling 00 generally meant a winning throw.*

Haiku on the Hunter and the Hunted

Caterpillar creeping
The swift birds mock your slow pace.
Do they know your twig?

Swift and hard I stoop.
Seize prey in freedom. Hunter,
Your lure's not for me.

September 26, 1980

The Falconer

Ferocious hawk tears swiftly with her beak
All who dare come near and yet are weak
Angry eyes strike first, then angry talons
In warning: Do not tip the falcon's balance.
Who then would guess that beating fast and fierce
That vicious hawk's heart harbors love and fear?
Fear first: the love into men's heart would pierce
Demanding truth as stark as falcon's tears
Which men have seen as nothing but attack
And so in self-defense they've stricken back.
But then a falconer came and saw the love
Called down the hawk from soaring heights above
    Now tamed—not beaten—by the falconer's fire
    The gentled hawk soars confidently higher.

July 12, 1989
Honest to the bare metal myself, I want others around me to be reasonably honest. I was often disappointed.

Cycles and circles

The Falconer II

And then the falconer came, and saw, and gentled
Ferocious hawk whose angry eyes would glare
At all who came, and with her talons raised
Dare who would approach her any closer
But falconer's hands are large and warm and gentle
And strong enough to hold a falcon near
No damage done discourages his purpose
Intentions are for loving, making dear.
He sees the loving heart that beats so fast
And fierce because she flies so near the sun.
The sun demands full truth if love must last
And all a falcon's deeds are cleanly done.
    And so too must the falconer himself be:
    A man of strength and truth and fierce pity.

July 12, 1989

The Debt

Echoes of the horrors I have done
Surround me with the fear
of living them from the other side.

The child is too precious,
I am too vulnerable,
and will do anything
that strength and integrity enable
to keep her safe, whole, free
an unshattered spirit.

My awakening magic
rouses in answer to unvoiced suspicions
Vague shadows
formless, terrifying.
The known danger is no easier to face,
and I fear to put words to, a name on,
what terrifies the most.

I have done it all, even that
and that
And have paid the many painful years
And lives
To be free of all those deeds.
I started the slow climb up
from the holocaust
a million years ago
And have given my life once
for each of theirs
Until peace finally settled
After one last throw of the cosmic dice
Turning my attention to the finer details.
Am I so hard to teach?

The pain of loving
And not being loved
Of a child wanting a mother, a father,
And having none:
I know these well
It aches in my bones

Cycles and circles

A knowledge deeper than blood.
I know what I did.
Remember it clearly.
Thought I did right
Out of ignorance, not knowing that they were me:
father, mother, sister, brother
Child
And what they suffered at my hands
I suffered, until the lesson was iron in my bones.
The agony, when it is yours
Makes the deed unthinkable.

September 7, 1990

How do you keep your child safe, when you know what people are capable of when their consciouis minds are disconnected from their souls? As Desmond Tutu and his daughter, Mpho Tutu say in their book, Made for Goodness *(HarperOne, 2011), "opting for the easy wrong may save the body, but it kills the soul."*

The Hounds

How long will you seek vengeance?
You say I don't understand
But I do.
Uneasiness traces my skin
every time you bring your prey to bay
And worry him, in joy
With your sharp bloody teeth
Until he dies, satisfyingly, painfully.
I'm sorry! I shout inside.
I am guilty too.
And though many slow years have passed
More than you imagine
I still lie awake at night
sleepless and still
Terrified at a nameless dark
That holds me by my willing throat
And whispers vengeance, vengeance in my ears.

September 7, 1990
A continuation of conversation cycle begun byt "The Debt" on page 146. The sequel to this poem is "The Effrontery of Time" on page 149. This poem was inspired, if inspired is the correct word, by reading about how Nazi war criminals are still being hunted down. I am in no way condoning Nazis or the damage they've done, but we can't find peace if hate is all we carry in our hearts. After writing my book on forgiveness, The Forgiving Lifestyle: How to Forgive Everyone (Including Yourself) *(Athena Star Press, 2014), I was invited to a radio show led by a Holocaust survival. He asked me if Nazis should be forgiven. I said yes. Forgiveness doesn't mean saying what was done is right or okay, because it wasn't. It just means that you're releasing a burden on your heart.*

The Effrontery of Time

Yet what can happen that hasn't before?
Feeling the fire's eager impatient embrace
Too demanding to remain whole in
So that instead your body
And those of your six companions
Dissolve into fine air:
What can that have felt like?
And what worse things
have already happened?

Yet that is past
And the fine moment of now
In its perfection
Is inviolate
Inviolable
Invincible.
And I am content.

September 7, 1990
A continuation of the conversation cycle begun with "The Debt" on page 146. This one is about one of my daughter's related lifetimes.

Wild Mustard I

It didn't go well
And I know why
Despite a smile that lit the sky
His mouth at rest said nothing good
And to my soul he fed—wormwood.

January 28, 1994
The first in my Wild Mustard cycle. Mustard grows wild throughout much of California; in Northern California, the wide fields of yellow are as familiar a sight as the oaks scattered on the inland sides of the coastal hills along Highway 101. Alas, lovely though it is, mustard is an invasive species, first brought to Alta California by the Spanish missionaries. (If you've heard otherwise, know that archaeologists have found mustard seeds in adobe bricks at Spanish missions.)

Wild Mustard II

Bitter, twisted, rank
When left in the fields too long—
Wild mustard can be sweet when harvested young,
But I was too late.

January 28, 1994

Wild Mustard III

Don't ask the wild geese where they're going
Don't ask me to wait or stay here
It isn't too late for the world and me
But it's too late to make up for your fear.

January 28, 1994
If fear freezes you in your tracks for too long, you have to catch the next train.

Wild Mustard IV

All right
Maybe I expected too much
And maybe you led me to
And maybe I allowed you to lead me
And maybe we could go on forever laying blame
When the only real issue here is trust and desire.
If you trusted me more
Or I trusted you less
If you desired this more
Or I wanted it less
We might have met halfway between;
We might have harvested wild mustard
And fresh spring water
Instead of finding ourselves
In a waterless garden
Where nothing can grow
Except bitterness and rank weeds.

January 28, 1994

A more conversational, understanding, and forgiving poem on the same topic as the others in the Wild Mustard cycle. Young wild mustard greens. steamed, are delicious.

Wild Mustard V

Ravens have a way of telling
Of spring and the wild mustard.
When I was young, I ran yelling,
To see the wild blackbirds fly.

Wild, now, to see the ravens
In the telling mustard spring
Enclosed by walls and those so craven
They fear to see the ravens fly.

When I was a child, no one was telling
Of magic and the wild spring
Now mustard blooms and I run yelling
I dare to hope, and so dreams fly.

November 15, 1996
I don't know whether to consider this a part of the Wild Mustard cycle, since in this poem the wild mustard actually refers to the real plant. But in the sense that it brings the cycle to a positive conclusion, I think it does belong. In the second-to-last line, "blooms" is a verb, not a noun.

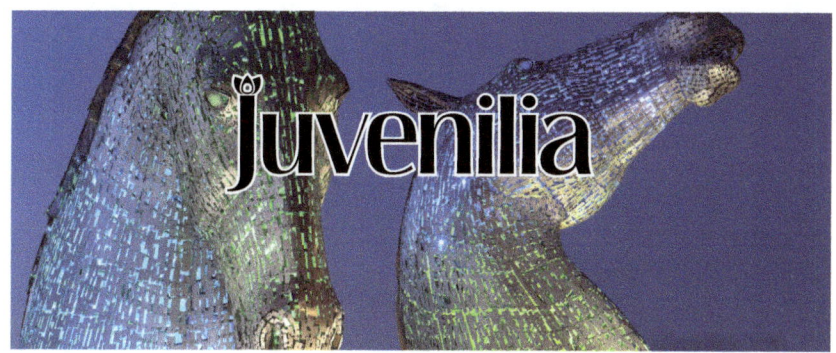

Juvenilia

I was astounded and delighted to discover the term "juvenilia," which means those things we write when we are young. It is a completely understandable term, which in one stroke excuses us of all those bad poems we wrote in our youth, while allowing us to keep some of them anyway, just in case someone, somewhere, actually likes our early work. A masterful use of the language, perfect for poetry.

You might notice in this collection that my juvenilia (that is, those poems that survived; I gave a merciful burial to many) extends rather far into my adult life. (And ditched another while preparing these poems for publication.) What can I say? I matured slowly.

When I moved to the desert in my mid-twenties, I started to write about my unusual and mystical experiences. Almost everything I wrote before then I consider juvenilia. Not quite all—and those few that stood the test of time are in other parts of this collection.

On the other hand, I've written some poems since my youth that nonetheless qualify for juvenilia. Becoming an adult is a process, not an event, and sometimes the waters flow backward.

Diamonds in the Rough

I
ask you
      to
accept
           the
                    roughnesses
in my character.
Time will smooth them.

Being what we are
we can only grow better
with age.

May 21, 1975
This poem is one of the very few where I used formatting as part of the poem. I'm still not sure whether this qualifies as a poem. A good poem is still poetry no matter how it's formatted; prose, no matter how well written, isn't poetry even when formatted as a poem.

Juvenilia

The Kiss

Hot biscuits and honey
And I think of you—
Salty-sweet in my mouth.

April 5, 1976
Despite the title, some people think this poem is about something other than a kiss. It isn't, and never was.

Driftwood

We could be very much in love
If you let yourself.
But you love that illusion of freedom called fear
Far too much.
I consider: Should I leave you?
I am bound to you
Bound with ties stronger than you can imagine
Or, imagining, want.
Like the sea I can't help myself
And I (in a hundred little ways)
Throw bits of myself
Large waves of myself
Before you.
And like the land
Eternally accustomed to such priceless homage
You return but rocks and sand
And turn your fairest face elsewhere.

1976

The Replacement

Occasionally
Though it has been months since you died
I look upon the new one
(Content in her new home
Pregnant
Full of life)
      So like, yet unlike you
And again I feel my heart warp with your loss.
Again I cry.

1976

This is about Rough (his sister was Ready—don't look at me, I didn't name them; my brothers did), a cat who died far too young.

Shoshannah in Winter

Sweet Shoshannah, graceful lily
Entwined in silvery waterfalls of tinsel icicles
The contrast on her jet fur
is beautiful.

Silver icicles
Contrasted with warm jet fur
Cat displays herself.

December 30, 1976
Two variations on one image. Shoshannah was a lovely tuxedo cat. By the way, never put tinsel on your tree if you have cats. I was lucky Shoshannah didn't try to eat it.

Phoenix Lays an Egg

I suppose I need no season
Or excuse for me to say
Although you are a tyrant
I love your charming way
Despite your lack of scruples
Your compassion warms my heart
Inflexible? You made the word
And polished well the art.
Yet now and then you do unbend
Enough to show you're human.
I could go on—the list is long—
Suffice it but to say
Your paradoxes interest me
And that is why I stay.

April 8, 1977

A part of the Phoenix cycle, but a little too bouncy to match the tone of the other poems in the cycle. Re-reading this poem from the distance of decades, I realize this poem explains how abusive people keep others in a relationship with them. Some part of me knew it then, but it took decades to suss it out and stop letting people like that into my life.

Song of a Psychology Student

For I will consider my rat Riffraffery.
For his fur is sleek and pale.
For his whiskers are long, and his eyes bright.
For his feet are nimble, as is his mind—they better be
For I will make him perform wondrous deeds.
For he can leap from place to place on command.
For he can ascend or descend rat mountains.
For he can traverse narrow rods.
For he can quickly tread a maze, and come out safely.
For he accomplishes all with a will
For I will then get an "A" in my psych class.

May 1, 1977
Riffing off the Jeoffry portion of Christopher Smart's (1722-1771) "Jubilate Agno" (in which he wrote in praise of his cat; the first line being "For I will consider my Cat Jeoffry," and each sebsequent line beginning with "For"), I wrote this poem about my college roommate and her friends, who were taking psychology classes in which they had to train rats. It's meant to be lighthearted.

Realization

I thought at first that it was just a crush
That made my heart feel warmer at your sight
I laughed it off and felt there was no rush—
Soon I'd forget, and all would be set right.
But years have passed, and still I wake from dreams
Of you and me in more than friendly way
I long for you, and yet it only seems
That you don't care for me, to my dismay.
I write this sonnet now to clear my soul
Knowing full well you'll never find out who
Has written such in manner that is droll.
Your heart lies elsewhere, yet I still love you.
    One day my heart will once again be mine
    For now I yield and send this valentine.

February 1978

In a scene in one of the Indiana Jones movies, Indiana is adored by his many female students. When I saw the movie in 1981, I laughed at that scene, because I'd taken classes from an anthropology professor at Santa Clara University who was the real Indiana. Every woman (and a few men) in his classes, which were always packed, had a crush on him. I wasn't an exception. Some of the more mischievous in the class would stack the chalk in the chalk tray in such a manner that the professor would brush against it, knocking the chalk to the floor so he would have to bend over in his tight pants to pick up the chalk. When I was in graduate school and therefore, I hoped, safe from suspicion, I sent this poem anonymously to the professor for Valentine's Day, 1978. If by some remote chance he reads this poem and remembers the card, the jig is up.

Vice Versa

We spar
Knowing best where to stab
Being so alike.
Sharing the same traits
Yet taking turns at showing them:
When one feels the most precise
Full of tidy places-for-things
The other strews debris
About floor and couch.
The moon changes
Or something
And roles reverse.
Now the once-messy shakes head
In self-righteous criticism.
      — I just cleaned —
      — So? — the insolent reply
And anger sparks
Between those with least cause.

August 1978
Compatibility is far more important to relationships than some of us realize.

Companions

Come—I can guide you
Lifting your foot over the rocks
Or around them
While you tell me of the clouds.
Or, we can turn
And I will reveal butterflies
And show you how to join them
In delicacy of movement.
I will show you how to touch things lightly
Without clumsy destruction
While you tell me of the intricate structure
And the wonder of tiny veins
Pulsing life to the now green, now blue
Powdery petals that give flight
To such strange bodies.

August 1978

Someone who thoughtlessly and unintentionally crushes things still crushes things. You can learn empathy, but only if you want to.

Anniversary of Realization

I did not betray you
Did you betray me?
Some long-ago lifetime
Shared by we three.
The memory lonely
Is all on my side
You've forgotten our shared love
Involved in your pride.
Who renounced whom?
I think it was thee
Though time has confused things—
It could have been me.
And was all the anguish
The result of real acts
Or did our minds hide truth
And just make up facts?
Our lives as they stand now
Are too far apart
We cannot meet head-on
Though sharing like art.
I will not betray you
Nor you betray me
I, for my love
And you—will not see.

February 1978
Some months after I wrote "Realization" (page 163), I remembered a related lifetime that cleared up the mystery for me.

Juvenilia

His Song

A woman of power whose grasp was weak
    I left her in dust and tears
A Viking maid whose mead was sweet
    I promised her all my years.

November 12, 1979
Written from the point of view a young person who enjoyed playing with women's hearts.

To the King of Beasts

So
Here you come
As I long ago predicted
Tomcat whiskers slicked and clean
Ears eagerly forward.

God spare me from your pounce.

So, whose heart do you rip today
By courting the past?

I'll have none of it.
Go find another for your game.
I won't allow you
To turn me into a symbol
For her to hate and you to worship
Directing all attention away from your own
Basic
Lack.

September 25, 1980

A Welcome and Invitation

Complete the picture
Frame my life
Bring balance and wholeness
Permanence.
I am here for you.
The images may shift
But the colors will remain:
Bright yellow joy
Deep blue satisfaction
Gentle pinkness
Rainbow love.

May 12, 1981

Words

I know sometimes words
Say least—
Your happy eyes,
Warm eyes around me
Holding me close to your unsteady heart—
Are love in a better form
Than words.
But I am a poet
Which is to say
I demand of words more
Than casual communication
More than statements, made once and never again.
Some words bear repeating.
My poet's heart craves words of praise
Where words of hate once etched their acid scorn.
Woo me with words, those unsteady messengers:
Words help to make this lasting dream more true.

1981 or 1982
Some people are honest enough to not put into words that which isn't true.

Juvenilia

The Persistence of Love

Anger comes, some nights
When I lie awake from slights
Given me down the years of life
From all the fools I've known
Who've taken what I've shown
To be a rare and precious gift of love
(Not just the men, but all
Whose minds were just as small)
And scorned it as a worthless piece of shit.

The poisoning was subtle
I could make no good rebuttal
Until almost too late I saw the danger.

Though I still struggle with those ghosts
Who rise and jeer and boast
Of how they once had had the best of me
Yet still my heart resists
And still my love persists
In pushing back the boundaries of their hate.

November 18, 1982
Really, everyone is trying their best, but to do what?

Fallen Star

All the times I've talked with you
Asking what you meant to do
All the times, the love we shared
This my question: "Do you care?"

All the love I've shared with you
Stringless, happy, giving, true
This is what I've learned from you:
Silence is an answer too.

Lack the courage, lack the grace
To say "It's over" to my face?
Know that I'll accept from you
That silence is an answer too.

September 28, 1984
Although this may sound like a poem about a romance, it's addressed to someone I once thought was my friend. An unfaithful husband and a lonely, libidinous friend was a bad mix. When I tried to talk with her to salvage the friendship, I got the door slam. I wrote this poem while still sad and angry at the double betrayal.

Translation

When studying Old English in 1974, I translated "The Battle of Brunanburh," a poem published in the 937 CE ***Anglo-Saxon Chronicle***. The poem commemorates a significant battle fought somewhere in Britain, no one knows where.

Here's what we think we know.

In 927 CE, Æthelstan, King of England, defeated Viking forces. After the Viking defeat, Constantine II, King of Scotland; Constantine's son-in-law Olaf Guthfrithson, King of Dublin; and Owain I, King of Strathclyd (where the native language was a form of old Welsh, though the land was further north than Wales) made a peace treaty with Æthelstan and accepted him as their lord.

The treaty didn't prevent Constantine, Olaf (called Anlaf in the poem), and Owain from constantly fighting each other, an ever-popular sport that's provided fodder for many a story and song over the millennia.

Peace with Æthelstan reigned until 934 CE, when Æthelstan invaded Scotland. His reasons are unknown, but early sources claim it was because Constantine violated the 927 peace treaty.

Constantine didn't like being invaded, so three years later, in 937, Constantine persuaded Olaf and Owain to set aside their differences to fight Æthelstan, with the hope of defeating Æthelstan forever. (Perhaps it took Constantine those three years to persuade the other men, or took all three that much time to gather their forces, or both.)

The resulting day-long battle, memorialized in "The Battle of Brunanburh," was brutal, fierce, and bloody. Æthelstan's forces won. In the same year, someone recorded the poem in ***Anglo-Saxon Chronicle***.

My translation is mostly literal, not poetic, retaining as much as possible the flavor and wording of the original.

One characteristic of Old English poetry was the use of stock phrases called kennings. Kennings were shorthand phrases that carried understood meanings. For example, the kenning hamora lafan (sometimes shown as lafum), which translates literally as "hammer leavings," was understood to mean swords. It may help to know that the f was pronounced like a v, so lafan is promounced more like lahvan. Try saying that out loud, and you can hear the word "leaving."

I recommend that you look up YouTube videos of people reciting the poem in Old English. You'll be amazed at how many Old English words are still understandable when pronounced.

I had translated the entire poem, but my translation of the last 15 lines went on walkabout sometime in the intervening decades.

After my translation, I've included the full original poem, which you can find, among many other places, at http://people.ucalgary.ca/~mmcgilli/ASPR/a10.1.html.

I make no claim to my translation being perfect, and I would expect scholars will be tempted to pick it apart. But I'm proud of the fact that I once knew Old English well enough to read and translate not just this, but many other Old Enligh poems.

The Battle of Brunanburh (translation)

Here Athelstan, king, lord of earls,
Ring-giver to warriors, and his brother also,
Eadmund noble-one, for long in glory
struck at battle swords' edges

around Brunanburh. The shielding walls cleaved they,
hewed they linden shields with hammer-leavings, swords sharp
of the sons of Eadward; of befittingly noble descent they,
from a line of warriors, that they at battles oft
with the loathed ones together each, land defended,

hordes and homes. The hated fell,
Scots and Vikings
Fey, they fell. Fields wet flowed
with warrior's blood (from) after sun-up
to morning tide, as the glorious star

glided over the lands (God's candle bright,
forever his) until that noble creation
settled to its seat. There lay warriors, many,
by spears undone, men of the North
over shields shot, just as the Scottish also

weary, war-sated, lay. West Saxons rode forth
the entire day, picked companies of horsemen
on the track lay of the hated princes,
fugitives they grievously from behind
(slashed with) swords mill-sharp. Heroes, they refused not

bitter close combat; not one
(Of) those who, with the Viking lord Anlaf, over the sea-course
(sailing) on ships' bosoms land sought,
fey, to fight. Five lay dead
on those battle-places, likewise seven also

of Anlaf's earls, countless numbers of the

Vikings and Scots. Here became fugitive
the North-man's sovereign; direly constrained they him.
To the sailor's ship-prows (fled) what little was left of their host

Pressed they onto ships afloat, (their) king out departed
on the fallow flood, (his) life to save.
Just as there also the old campaigner amid their flight came
in(to) his homeland north, Constantine,
hoary warrior. Exult had he no reason to

in swords' fellowship; he was of his kins bereft.
Friends fell on the battlefield,
all slain on the battlefield, and his son abandoned
at the place of slaughter, wounded, ground to pieces,
(so young) by battle.

Boast had he no reason to.
Warrior, grizzle-haired, by swords slaughtered,
old malicious one, Anlaf (because of) that could boast no more.

Amid their survivors, laugh had they no reason to
that they in deeds of war had the better of it.
In battlefield's banner-collisions,
spear-encounters, men together permitted
weapon exchanges, that they on the slaughter-fields
with Eadward's descendants played.

Departed they the northmen of the nail-studded ships,
dejected spear survivors, on Dinges sea
over deep water Dublin sought.

(The last 15 lines of my translation, starting with "eft Iraland, æwiscmode," have been lost.)

The Battle of Brunanburh (original)

Her æþelstan cyning,   eorla dryhten,
beorna beahgifa,   and his broþor eac,
Eadmund æþeling,   ealdorlangne tir
geslogon æt sæcce   sweorda ecgum

ymbe Brunanburh.   Bordweal clufan,
heowan heaþolinde   hamora lafan,
afaran Eadweardes,   swa him geæþele wæs
from cneomægum,   þæt hi æt campe oft
wiþ laþra gehwæne   land ealgodon,

hord and hamas.   Hettend crungun,
Sceotta leoda   and scipflotan
fæge feollan,   feld dænnede
secga swate,   siðþan sunne up
on morgentid,   mære tungol,

glad ofer grundas,   godes condel beorht,
eces drihtnes,   oð sio æþele gesceaft
sah to setle.   þær læg secg mænig
garum ageted,   guma norþerna
ofer scild scoten,   swilce Scittisc eac,

werig, wiges sæd.   Wesseaxe forð
ondlongne dæg   eorodcistum
on last legdun   laþum þeodum,
heowan herefleman   hindan þearle
mecum mylenscearpan.   Myrce ne wyrndon

heardes hondplegan   hæleþa nanum
þæra þe mid Anlafe   ofer æra gebland
on lides bosme   land gesohtun,
fæge to gefeohte.   Fife lægun
on þam campstede   cyningas giunge,

sweordum aswefede,   swilce seofene eac
eorlas Anlafes,   unrim heriges,
flotan and Sceotta.   þær geflemed wearð

Norðmanna bregu,   nede gebeded,
to lides stefne   litle weorode;

cread cnear on flot,   cyning ut gewat
on fealene flod,   feorh generede.
Swilce þær eac se froda   mid fleame com
on his cyþþe norð,   Costontinus,
har hilderinc,   hreman ne þorfte

mæca gemanan;   he wæs his mæga sceard,
freonda gefylled   on folcstede,
beslagen æt sæcce,   and his sunu forlet
on wælstowe   wundun forgrunden,
giungne æt guðe.   Gelpan ne þorfte

beorn blandenfeax   bilgeslehtes,
eald inwidda,   ne Anlaf þy ma;
mid heora herelafum   hlehhan ne þorftun
þæt heo beaduweorca   beteran wurdun
on campstede   cumbolgehnastes,

garmittinge,   gumena gemotes,
wæpengewrixles,   þæs hi on wælfelda
wiþ Eadweardes   afaran plegodan.
Gewitan him þa Norþmen   nægledcnearrum,
dreorig daraða laf,   on Dinges mere

ofer deop wæter   Difelin secan,
eft Iraland,   æwiscmode.
Swilce þa gebroþer   begen ætsamne,
cyning and æþeling,   cyþþe sohton,
Wesseaxena land,   wiges hremige.

Letan him behindan   hræw bryttian
saluwigpadan,   þone sweartan hræfn,
hyrnednebban,   and þane hasewanpadan,
earn æftan hwit,   æses brucan,
grædigne guðhafoc   and þæt græge deor,

wulf on wealde.   Ne wearð wæl mare
on þis eiglande   æfre gieta
folces gefylled   beforan þissum
sweordes ecgum,   þæs þe us secgað bec,

Translation

ealde uðwitan, siþþan eastan hider
Engle and Seaxe up becoman,
ofer brad brimu Brytene sohtan,
wlance wigsmiþas, Wealas ofercoman,
eorlas arhwate eard begeatan.

Other Books by Marina E. Michaels

The Forgiving Lifestyle: How to Forgive Everyone (Including Yourself)

Delectable Desserts (volume 1 of the *Delicious Connections* cookbook series)

Recipes Your Mother Knew by Heart (volume 2 of the *Delicious Connections* cookbook series)

All available on Amazon worldwide

Did this book help you in some way? If so, I'd love to hear about it through your review on Amazon, Goodreads, Barnes and Noble, or any other site where you found this book. Honest reviews help readers find the right book for their needs.

www.ingramcontent.com/pod-product-compliance
Lightning Source LLC
Chambersburg PA
CBHW071313110426
42743CB00042B/1471